THEORETICAL WELFARE ECONOMICS

THEORETICAL WELFARE ECONOMICS

BY

J. DE V. GRAAFF

CAMBRIDGE
AT THE UNIVERSITY PRESS
1971

PUBLISHED BY
THE SYNDICS OF THE CAMBRIDGE UNIVERSITY PRESS
Bentley House, 200 Euston Road, London NW1 2DB
American Branch: 32 East 57th Street, New York, N.Y.10022

ISBN
0 521 05128 2 clothbound
0 521 09446 1 paperback

First published 1957
Reprinted 1964, 1967
First paperback edition 1967
Reprinted 1971

First printed in Great Britain by Spottiswoode, Ballantyne & Co. Ltd, London and Colchester
Reprinted, by Lithography, in Great Britain by
Hazell Watson & Viney Ltd,
Aylesbury, Bucks

CONTENTS

FOREWORD

If somebody asks me what modern welfare economics is about, I always recommend to them Graaff's *Theoretical Welfare Economics*. Less than 200 pages in length, the book has become a classic in our own time. And one test of its classical stature is the fact that one sees often, in contemporary books and journals, rediscoveries of results already contained in the book.

The welfare economics treated here is the culmination of a great tradition. By 1930 the ethical hedonism of Bentham, Sidgwick, Edgeworth, and Marshall had come under heavy attack by Gunnar Myrdal and Lionel (now Lord) Robbins as involving a-scientific interpersonal comparison of utility. Professor Abram Bergson of Harvard, while still a young graduate student, founded in a too-little known article in the 1938 *Quarterly Journal of Economics*, the modern theory of welfare economics. Introducing from outside of positive economics a social welfare function appropriate to a given set of ethical norms, Bergson was able to show what its maximization implied for observable economic variables. Bergson was thus able to avoid (or, alternatively, to include) the hedonistic summation of cardinal utilities, and at the same time to value at their true (limited) worth the Pareto-optimality necessary conditions that are themselves expressible independently of a social welfare function. So to speak, this put the narrow 'new welfare economics' of Pareto, Hotelling, A. P. Lerner, Kaldor, and Hicks in its proper place. The late Oskar Lange, of Poland and Chicago, I, and Graaff developed the Bergson foundations.

When I say that this kind of welfare economics has today swept the field, I wish to make clear that it is not true, as many used to believe, that Professor Kenneth Arrow of Stanford has proved 'the impossibility of a social welfare function'. What Arrow has proved in his pathbreaking 1951, *Social Choice and Individual Values*, is the impossibility of what I prefer to call 'a political constitution function', which would be able to resolve *any* interpersonal differences brought to it while at the same time satisfying certain reasonable and desirable axioms. This Arrow result is a basic theorem of what might be called 'mathematical politics' and throws new light on age-old conundrums of democracy. But it does not detract, I believe, from the Bergson formulations nor from the lasting value of the present work.

PAUL A. SAMUELSON
Institute Professor
Massachusetts Institute of Technology

May 1967

PREFACE

A fairly complete account of the formal theory of welfare economics will be found in the chapters that follow. I have striven to make the body of the text intelligible to non-mathematical readers, but occasional bits of symbolism seem somehow to have crept in. All sustained mathematical argument, however, is carefully segregated in appendices, which can be omitted without great loss. They deal chiefly with elementary maximization problems, and are likely to earn the scorn of both the professional mathematician and the workaday economist. The appendices follow the chapters to which they refer (Chapters II–IV and IX). A note on terminology follows this Preface.

My debt to the literature is far larger than the occasional footnote references to specific sources might seem to imply, but generally it is too diffused to enable me to make more detailed acknowledgement. I must, however, record here the extent to which I have drawn inspiration from the published work of Professor Paul A. Samuelson of the Massachusetts Institute of Technology. His remarkable theoretical insight has spared me much labour.

The many friends who have advised me on particular points are too numerous to mention individually; but some have given so generously of their time that I cannot simply include them in an omnibus acknowledgement. I recall with considerable pleasure a number of long conversations with Dr Lawrence R. Klein when, in the summer of 1948, he was visiting the Department of Applied Economics in Cambridge. Over the period of the next twelve months I benefited greatly from frequent discussions with Professor William J. Baumol of Princeton University, who was then working on similar problems at the London School of Economics. And in Cambridge itself I have had the constant help and advice of Professor R. F. Kahn, who has been responsible for the removal of countless errors from a first draft I ungraciously imposed upon him. For nearly two years he has read with singular patience almost everything I have written on economic matters, and the debt I owe him is too great to try to express. I must, however, state that neither he nor anyone else has seen the final versions of the chapters which follow, and that the many errors which undoubtedly remain are therefore entirely my own responsibility.

J. DE V. GRAAFF

NOTE ON TERMINOLOGY

The reader may find it useful to refer to the following brief explanations of some of the terms which are used in special senses in the text.

(1) W is the symbol used for a *social welfare function*. It is said to be of the *individualist type* if it depends on the individual utility indicators of a definite group of men (so that their individual preferences 'count'), and to be a *Pareto W* (or Paretian welfare function) if, being of the individualist type, a *cet. par.* increase in any one man's well-being increases social well-being.

(2) The *General Optimum* obtains whenever the 'correct' collection of goods is produced and 'correctly' distributed among the members of the group. (Rendering a productive service is to be regarded as consuming a negative amount of a good.) 'Correctness' is of course interpreted in terms of a particular W.

(3) The *marginal equivalences of the General Optimum* are the set of equalities and inequalities which must necessarily hold whenever any Pareto W attains a (constrained)† maximum.

(4) The social *production frontier* shows the maximum amount of any one output which it is possible to produce, given the amounts of all the other outputs (and regarding inputs as negative outputs).

(5) The *welfare frontier* shows how well off it would be possible (given the social production frontier, and assuming that there were no impediments of a political or practical nature) to make any one member of a definite group of men, given the levels of well-being to be enjoyed by each of the other members of the group.

(6) The *feasibility locus* shows how well off it is politically feasible to make any one member of a group, given the levels of well-being to be enjoyed by each of the other members.

(7) The *efficiency locus* shows how well off the various members of the group actually would be if lump-sum redistributions of wealth were to be made, starting from any position (inside or on

† The constraint being provided by the social production frontier.

the welfare frontier), in which society actually finds itself. It indicates the allocative efficiency of the economy.

(8) A social (or community) indifference curve of the *Scitovsky frontier* type shows the minimum amount of any one good, given the amounts of the others, necessary to keep each member of the group on a prescribed level of indifference.

(9) A social indifference curve of the *Bergson frontier* type shows the minimum amount of any one good, given the amounts of the others, necessary to maintain a given level of W.

(10) *Excessive* external effects in consumption exist whenever a larger collection of goods (i.e. a collection in which at least one good is increased in amount, and none decreased) fails to lead to a higher level of W, no matter how it is distributed.

[In (8)–(10), as in (2), rendering a productive service is to be regarded as consuming a negative amount of a good.]

CHAPTER I

INTRODUCTION

Theoretical welfare economics proceeds from a number of definite assumptions, factual and ethical, which are seldom stated explicitly. If their nature were more widely appreciated by professional economists, it is improbable that the conventional conclusions of welfare theory would continue to be stated with as little caution as is at present the custom. What is their nature? That will become clear as we proceed. Let us start by drawing a loose but convenient distinction between welfare theory and the other branches of economics.

WELFARE ECONOMICS AND POSITIVE ECONOMICS

What determines the price of wheat? Has the real national income increased? Should a protective tariff be placed on imports? These are all questions which economists have, at one time or another, investigated, and to which they are generally expected to be able to provide answers. The three questions are, however, of very different kinds. The first relates to *positive economics*. The answer is provided, more or less satisfactorily, by a body of theory which seeks to explain various phenomena in the world about us. The third relates to *welfare economics*—a normative subject, the nature of which it is our purpose to investigate.

The second question does not fall into either of these great divisions as readily as the first and the third. On the one hand, it could be argued that the term 'real national income' is a mere definition, devoid of normative significance, and that whether or not it has increased is a matter for empirical investigation alone. On the other hand, it could be objected that 'the real national income' is an emotive expression; and that to say that it has increased is to imply that the state of affairs thus described is approved, or in some sense thought to be good and desirable.†

† Dr I. M. D. Little, in particular, has been insistent on this point.

Professional economists, it is true, might train themselves to strip terms of their normative associations, and learn to regard the 'national income' as no more than 'that which this index measures'—in the same way that positivist psychologists define 'intelligence' as 'that which intelligence tests measure'. But it is too much to hope that the layman will do likewise; and so, if we agree (as I think we must) that words or phrases do in fact acquire emotive and recommendatory connotations, we must place questions of the second sort into the normative division, and look to welfare economics for their answers.

It would be fruitless to attempt a clear-cut dichotomy, but it is nevertheless important to get a rough idea of the essential differences between positive economics and welfare economics. The theoretical parts of the former, in so far as they possess any empirical content at all, provide us with theorems we can test against the facts they purport to explain—with propositions about the real world which can, at least in principle, be falsified and rejected, if not verified and established. That a rise in price will always choke off demand, is such a proposition. It can be (and in fact has been) refuted by observation of market phenomena. Nowadays we make reservations about expectations and inferior goods.

The propositions of welfare economics have a rather different content. They are logical deductions from a set of definitions and assumptions which may or may not themselves be realistic, and which may or may not be ethical in nature. Having defined welfare, for an individual or a group, and made various assumptions, we can deduce the conditions under which it will increase. If these conditions are fulfilled and welfare does not increase, it simply means that our assumptions are inappropriate. Thus far there is no difference between normative theory and positive theory. The difference arises when we actually try to discover whether or not welfare has in fact increased. For welfare (as we shall in due course define it) is not an observable quantity like a market price or an item of personal consumption. It is a bird of another sort. It is in practice, if not in principle, exceedingly difficult to test a welfare proposition. Just how great the difficulty is, the reader will have to decide for himself as he proceeds—it is essentially a matter on which private estimations will differ. But whether or not the difficulty is judged insuperable, one consequence of its mere existence is of the greatest importance.

The consequence is that, whereas the normal way of testing a theory in positive economics is to test its conclusions, the normal way of testing a welfare proposition is to test its assumptions. The significance of this should not be overlooked. In positive economics we can often simplify our assumptions as cavalierly as we please, being confident in the knowledge that their appropriateness will be tested when we come to apply the conclusions inherent in them to our observations of the world about us. In welfare economics we can entertain no such confidence. The result is that our assumptions must be scrutinized with care and thoroughness. Each must stand on its own feet. We cannot afford to simplify much. Nor can we blindly hope that two erroneous assumptions will somehow 'cancel out' and produce an acceptable conclusion—whereas in positive economics this procedure is as common as it is essential.† There the proof of the pudding is indeed in the eating. The welfare cake, on the other hand, is so hard to taste that we must sample its ingredients before baking.

If this much be granted, it is clear that the interest attaching to a theory of welfare depends almost entirely upon the realism and relevance of its assumptions, factual and ethical, in a particular historical context. One way of proceeding would therefore be to enumerate very briefly the assumptions necessary for the currently conventional conclusions, to indicate even more briefly how these conclusions are drawn, and then to spend the rest of the time evaluating the assumptions, one by one. Another would be to

† To give but a single example, if we assume *inter alia* that a man has a constant rate of time preference and that the marginal utility of consumption diminishes (two assumptions which are, in themselves, better described as 'non-testable' or 'meaningless' than as 'erroneous'), we can deduce that a sufficiently high rate of interest will always result in consumption being planned to grow through time. The conclusion is testable and may be acceptable, even if the assumptions from which it is derived are not. See J. de V. Graaff, 'Mr Harrod on Hump Saving', *Economica*, vol. XVII (1950), esp. pp. 88–90.

treat the matter historically, concentrating on *Dogmengeschichte*, and trying to rationalize the tacit acceptance of various assumptions in various periods. I shall adopt neither of these methods of exposition. The first is too formal; and not only have I come to feel that *Dogmengeschichte* has to be done in great detail to be worth doing at all, but to such an extent has the theme of social reform lent inspiration to even the theoretical work of economists of all periods that the dimensions of the task would be extraordinarily large.† Instead I shall develop the theory step by step under rather general assumptions, indicating from time to time the correspondence of their special cases to the conventional conclusions. Then I shall review in its light three contemporary controversies—about tariffs and the terms of trade, the pricing policy of public enterprises, and the valuation of social income. Finally I shall try to evaluate its broader significance.

Inevitably, much familiar ground will be covered, especially in the earlier stages. But the reader is asked to bear this patiently, as it is essential to some of the later developments. Throughout the emphasis will be on pure rather than applied theory. Even if we find (as we of course shall) that full employment, in a special sense, is a necessary condition for maximum welfare, we shall not pause to consider such topical questions as what sort of economic environment, or type of economic policy, is likely (from a theoretical point of view) to bring it about. Nor shall we turn very often to positive economics to ask to what extent our welfare criteria are likely to be satisfied in different economic systems. The 'problem of planning' is beyond our scope.

That is the scheme to be followed. Our field is closely circumscribed. We can best enter it by defining the sense in which we shall use the word 'welfare'.

INDIVIDUAL WELFARE: GENERAL AND ECONOMIC

Attempts have often been made, especially by natural scientists, to give some objective meaning to a person's 'welfare'. The daily

† For a very useful survey, see Hla Myint, *Theories of Welfare Economics* (London, 1948).

intake of calories, the integration of the personality (which some psychologists seem to think objective), longevity †—all these have been suggested at one time or another. We need not discuss them. Their diversity provides sufficient indication of their arbitrariness; and for quite a long time the economist's conception has in any case been a subjective one. Something to the effect that welfare is a state of mind, or that 'the elements of welfare are states of consciousness' ‡ is generally accepted. We shall accept it too; but we shall try to maintain an element of objectivity by linking individual welfare very closely to individual choice.

The matter can be put somewhat formally by saying that a person's welfare map is defined to be identical with his preference map—which indicates how he would choose between different situations, if he were given the opportunity for choice. To say that his welfare would be higher in A than in B is thus no more than to say that he would choose A rather than B, if he were allowed to make the choice.

There are of course many difficulties and ambiguities in this definition, but these we shall leave unanalysed until we come to the detailed discussion of Chapter III. For the moment it is sufficient to draw the classical distinction between general welfare and economic welfare. To Pigou the latter was that part of the former which could 'be brought directly or indirectly into relation with the measuring-rod of money'.§ His phrase is suggestive and helpful, but money turns out to be such an unsatisfactory measuring-rod in welfare problems that it is best avoided. Moreover, the impression may be created that there are 'segregable parts of states of mind which can be attributed to economic causes'.‖ So we shall instead regard a person's choices, or general welfare, as determined by a large number of variables, some of which have traditionally interested economists and some of which have not. Those which have we shall call *economic variables*. Welfare

† Radhakamal Mukerjee, *The Political Economy of Population* (London, 1943).
‡ A. C. Pigou, *The Economics of Welfare* (4th ed., London, 1932), p. 10.
§ *Op. cit.* p. 11.
‖ I. M. D. Little, 'The valuation of Social Income', *Economica*, vol. XVI (1949), p. 15.

economics then proceeds on the assumption that the non-economic ones all remain unchanged. They can be thought of as exogenous—that is, as influencing the economic variables without being influenced by them. Thus the weather is clearly an exogenous or non-economic variable, affecting individual choices but unaffected by them.

A difficulty emerges when a variable which has not traditionally interested economists cannot be regarded as exogenous in this sense. For instance, it might be argued that there is a mutual interaction between forms of social organization (such as the family or the church) and economic variables. That religious beliefs affect personal consumption is clear. If there is just this one-way causal relationship no problem arises in examining the effect of a change in consumption on general welfare, religious beliefs remaining unchanged. But if they are themselves influenced by personal consumption—if a man's devotion depends in the long run on whether he is well fed or starving—we cannot pretend that they do remain unchanged. The two hang together. And since the economist has very little to say about the welfare significance of religious beliefs he can say equally little about personal consumption.

Pigou avoided the difficulty by what he called a 'judgement of probability' and asserted that 'qualitative conclusions about the effect of an economic cause upon economic welfare will hold good also of the effect on total welfare',† unless there is specific evidence to the contrary. Such a judgement is not easy to accept. If we really do not know, we do not know—and there is no point in pretending that we have enough information for a probability judgement. The only satisfactory solution is to assume quite explicitly that our non-economic variables are exogenous in the full sense of the term. This we shall do, but in Chapter VIII we shall have occasion to question the validity of the assumption. In the meantime we shall abbreviate 'economic welfare' to 'welfare' and try to guard against attaching a spurious generality to our conclusions.

† *Op. cit.* p. 20.

GROUP WELFARE

It would be very convenient if we could define group welfare in exactly the same way as individual welfare—if we could say that it would be higher in A than in B whenever A would be chosen. Unfortunately, however, groups do not frequently make unanimous choices. Majorities, it is true, often agree; but we are interested in the welfare of the whole group, not just the majority. We must adopt a different approach.†

The transition from individual to group (or social) welfare can be made in at least three ways, which lead to three qualitatively different concepts. Each presupposes that the group in which we are interested, and whose welfare is in some sense to be maximized, is clearly demarcated. To this matter we return in Chapter VI. Here we need only note that the demarcation must be made.‡

The first concept of group welfare I shall call the *paternalist*, as it is completely divorced from the preferences of the individual members of the group. The state, or paternalist authority, has its own ideas about welfare which may or may not take cognisance of economic factors such as the size and distribution of the national income. There is thus very little that the economist can say until he knows just what the state conceives welfare to be, and how much importance it proposes to attribute to its economic elements.

Indeed, the paternalist conception would hardly be worth mentioning were it not that an approach very similar to it is employed in the last part of Chapter XI, where we discuss the valuation of social income. Each person is assumed to value the whole social income, taking into account both its composition and its distribution; and the problem of social income is viewed as the

† The methods of mathematical logic have been applied to the whole problem of social choice in a most elegant way by Kenneth J. Arrow, *Social Choice and Individual Values* (John Wiley & Sons, Inc., New York, 1951). He brings out very clearly the limitations of a definition of social welfare in terms of social choice.

‡ If we fail to make the demarcation we may find ourselves asking, as Professor R. F. Kahn has done, in what way unemployed labour differs from unemployed land. The answer is of course that, whereas we are usually concerned with the welfare of labourers, we are not usually concerned with the welfare of units of land—whatever that may mean. See R. F. Kahn, 'Some Notes on Ideal Output', *Economic Journal*, vol. XLV (1935), p. 1.

problem of 'weighing' one man's valuation against another's. Like the paternalist state, each man can perform his valuation according to his own lights, and need not necessarily pay regard to the preferences of others. Each man in turn is, in effect, regarded as the paternalist authority.

Moreover, as we shall see in Chapter III, it is often the custom to think of the group as comprising a number of households, rather than a number of individual men. It is not immediately clear that any other meaning can be given to 'the choice of the household' than 'the choice of the head of the household'. If this is the case, some form of paternalist—or maternalist—idea of welfare must be applied *within* each household, no matter what is applied to the group of households as a whole.

The second concept of group welfare hinges on what has come to be known as the impossibility of making interpersonal comparisons of well-being. If these interpersonal comparisons cannot be made, the welfare of the group is clearly no more than a heterogeneous collection of individual welfares. If some men are made better off, and none worse off, group welfare rises; if some are made worse off, and none better off, it falls. But if some are made better off and some worse off we just do not know what has happened to the welfare of the group.

This is essentially the concept employed by Pareto † and his followers (especially Barone ‡). It leads naturally to their celebrated criterion for a maximum of group welfare: that it must not be possible to make any one man better off without making at least one other worse off.

The third concept emerges when we recognize that economists do not really mean that interpersonal comparisons are 'impossible'. All that they mean is that they cannot be made without judgements of an essentially ethical nature.§ If we make these

† Vilfredo Pareto, *Manuel d'Économie Politique* (2nd ed., Paris, 1929), pp. 617 ff.

‡ Enrico Barone, 'Il ministerio della produzione nello stato colletivista', *Giornale degli Economisti*, (1908), pp. 267–93 and 391–414, translated in F. A. Hayek (ed.) *Collectivist Economic Planning* (London, 1935).

§ Lionel Robbins, 'Interpersonal Comparisons of Utility', *Economic Journal*, vol. XLVIII (1938), pp. 635–41.

explicitly, we can formalize them in the shape of a Bergson social welfare function of the individualist type.† We shall represent the function by $W(u^1, ..., u^\nu)$, where the u's are the utility functions (or choice indicators) of the ν men comprising the group. It either summarizes or implies a detailed set of ethical judgements regarding the way in which one man's welfare is to be 'added' to another's. Since we shall make frequent use of W in the chapters that follow, it is as well to say something of its rationale straight away.‡

If we had to wait until we were actually given a detailed set of ethical judgements before we could say anything about group welfare, we should not get very far. Yet we do not want to specify W in detail ourselves, for then interest in our conclusions would be limited to those who shared the detailed judgements of the W we happened to specify. What we want to do is to see how much of interest we can say that will be true for a wide range of welfare functions, or on the basis of ethical propositions of a broad and commonly accepted kind. Clearly, we cannot hope to say anything that will be true for *all* welfare functions—for to assert the contrary would be to assert that the antithesis of a particular ethical proposition is not itself an ethical proposition. So we shall confine ourselves to those which satisfy the *Pareto condition*. That is to say, we shall confine ourselves to W's for which an increase in one man's welfare, the welfare of each of the other members of

† Abram Bergson (Burk), 'A Reformulation of Certain Aspects of Welfare Economics', *Quarterly Journal of Economics*, vol. LII (1938), pp. 310–34. The phrase 'of the individualist type' is inserted because a Bergson social welfare function can, in principle, be set up to describe the views of a paternalist authority—the variables upon which it depends need not necessarily be the individual utility indicators.

‡ Dr Little has criticized the Bergson social welfare function approach on the grounds that from it 'practical welfare conclusions can only be deduced if an "ideal" distribution of real income is given', and that 'on this formulation the only sufficient condition for an increase in welfare, which is implied, is that all the "optimum" conditions, together with an "optimum" real income distribution, be put into operation together. It is Utopia or nothing.' (I. M. D. Little, 'The Foundations of Welfare Economics', *Oxford Economic Papers*, vol. I, no. 2 (1949), pp. 237 and 228, n.). Both the quoted statements are incorrect. If we are given a social welfare function, it does not have to tell us which distribution is 'ideal': it merely has to order different distributions. Moreover, with its aid we can compare *any* two situations, whether optimal or not. There is nothing remotely Utopian about it.

the group remaining the same, leads to an increase in social welfare.

It will be convenient to have a name for welfare functions which satisfy this condition, and we shall call them *Paretian*. The totality of such functions we shall then refer to as the Paretian *class* of welfare functions. It has one rather important property. Anything we can say that will be true for *every* member of the class will remain true if we suddenly revert to our second concept of group welfare by proclaiming the illegitimacy of interpersonal comparisons. This is so because the only characteristic which the members of the class have in common is that they satisfy the Pareto condition: that it is a good thing to make one man better off if nobody else is made worse off. No statement made on this basis requires the making of any interpersonal comparisons at all. It requires a very broad ethical judgement ('that it is a good thing . . .'), but nothing else.

The classical notion of the Cambridge school, that group welfare is simply the sum of the cardinal† utilities of the men comprising the group, leads to a very elementary Paretian welfare function. Here W takes the form:

$$W(u^1, \ldots, u^\nu) = u^1 + \ldots + u^\nu.$$

It is clear that anything we can say without making interpersonal comparisons (that is, anything we can say for *every* welfare function satisfying the Pareto condition) will be applicable to the Cambridge W. The reverse is, however, naturally untrue.

The range of ethical systems describable by Paretian welfare functions is extremely large, and it is natural to suspect that it will prove too large to enable us to say much of interest. On this it will be easier to form an opinion at a later stage. At the moment it is sufficient to draw attention to a wider problem. The function W is not in fact *given* to us. Can it be *formed*? That is to say, can we somehow distil the various ethical beliefs of the members of a community into a consistent system, suitable for our purposes and capable of telling us how to 'add' one man's welfare to another's?

† Discussion of the general problem of 'measurement'—whether of individual or group welfare—is postponed for Chapter III.

The answer clearly depends on the extent to which we require *detailed* ethical judgements. If fairly broad ones will do (such as those implied by the Pareto criterion: that it is a good thing to make one man better off if no one is made worse off), then we can reasonably hope to find sufficient consilience of opinion in a moderately homogeneous society to enable us to proceed. But if agreement is required on matters of detail as well as on matters of principle, we are unlikely to be so lucky.

One of the things we must continually bear in mind, therefore, is the *specificity* of the ethical assumptions we find ourselves making. We want to keep them as broad as possible, so that interest in our conclusions may be widespread. But we also want them to be detailed enough to yield some conclusions. This is a theme to which we shall frequently return, and eventually we must try to give a balanced judgement on the matter.

THE CLASSIFICATION OF COMMODITIES

There remain two matters which it will be helpful to clear out of the way before embarking. The first has to do with the classification of commodities. It is natural to think of the varieties or qualities of the various commodities (in which term we include the services of the factors of production) as constituting a continuous range. There are, at least conceptually, an infinite number of grades of wheat, sizes of shoe or types of labour. Any classification we may make into a finite number of homogeneous classes is bound to be arbitrary. It is of course true that at a given time a definite number of more or less homogeneous commodities will be being produced in any society, but in welfare theory we are interested too in what *could* be produced.

If we stipulate, as indeed we must, that two physically identical objects available on different dates are different goods, the same problem arises in a more acute form. For time is clearly continuous, and the conventional habit of slicing it up into periods of finite length clearly unsatisfactory. Yet that is what we shall do.

It is in principle perfectly possible to avoid classifying the continuous range into a finite number of homogeneous classes. It is admittedly cumbersome—leading mathematically to problems involving functionals, rather than functions of a finite number of variables†—but it is perfectly possible. My reasons for not following this course are threefold. Firstly, there is the consideration of simplicity; secondly, that of conventionality—it would not be easy to compare our results with those usually reached if we recognized no such thing as a homogeneous commodity; and, thirdly, we can put forward a plausible but specious argument to the effect that by making the classification sufficiently fine we can achieve any desired degree of approximation. This sounds well enough, and it is true that the number of commodities can be exceedingly large, as long as it is finite. But it is probably specious, because just what we are approximating to is not very clear when ordinal quantities like welfare are involved. It nevertheless emphasizes an important point; and, as we shall see, our classification must in any case satisfy certain criteria of fineness to be developed in Chapters II and III.

It should be noted that our procedure does not preclude consideration of such problems as product differentiation, the welfare aspects of which have often been stressed.‡ It merely assumes that the differentiation takes place in discrete steps, and treats the mounting of each step as the advent of a new commodity. We shall therefore not discuss the matter specifically. Once we have agreed on a classification of commodities, it emerges as a particular case of the general problem of 'ideal' output.

We shall not, however, go to the opposite extreme of admitting that our finite number of commodities comprises a finite number of indivisible units. Mathematically, that would take us into the topology of sets of points. Instead we shall assume that each commodity is perfectly divisible and that its amount can vary continuously, so that we can apply the familiar methods of the

† Cf. Louis M. Court, 'Entrepreneurial and Consumer Demand Theories for Commodity Spectra', *Econometrica*, vol. IX (1941), pp. 135–62 and 241–97.

‡ Stephen Enke, 'Resource Malallocation within Firms', *Quarterly Journal of Economics*, vol. LXIII (1949), pp. 572–6; E. H. Chamberlin, *The Theory of Monopolistic Competition* (5th ed., Cambridge, Mass., 1946), pp. 214 ff.; also R. F. Kahn, 'Some Notes on Ideal Output', *Economic Journal*, vol. XLV (1935), pp. 1–35.

differential calculus. Only in Chapter VII shall we drop this pretence.

THE OBSERVING ECONOMIST

The last matter to clear out of the way has to do with an expository device we shall occasionally employ. We shall assume the existence of an omniscient being—the observing economist—who possesses whatever information we may require about tastes, techniques, the future, and anything else. The whole procedure will hardly commend itself to a solipsist, but it will nevertheless prove convenient.

The information put at our disposal in this way we hold with *certainty*—it is *correct* information. But the same does not apply to the members of the community we shall be studying. Until we reach Chapter VIII we shall abstract from uncertainty on their part, but we shall occasionally remark on the consequences of their expectations being wrong. Whether a man can fail to experience uncertainty when his expectations persistently turn out to be mistaken is a question I shall avoid.

CHAPTER II

TECHNOLOGY

A large and important part of welfare economics can be pursued at the engineering level. The present chapter gives a brief survey of some of the well-known results concerning the 'optimal' organization of production. The only value judgement required in the analysis is that more of any output, or less of any input, is *cet. par.* a good thing.

To emphasize that we are dealing with purely technological relationships, we shall eschew the use of money. Costs, prices and

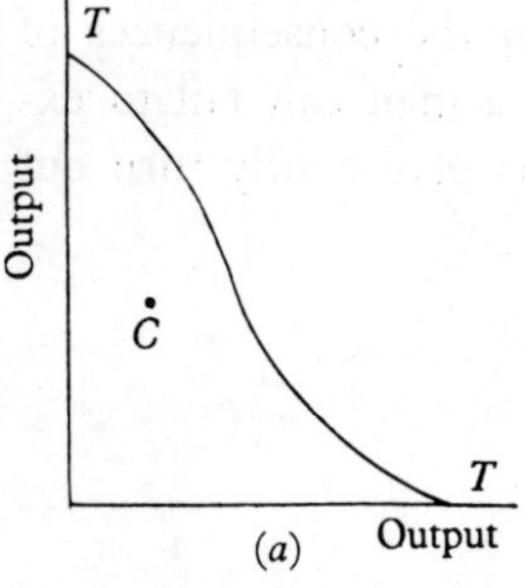

(*a*)

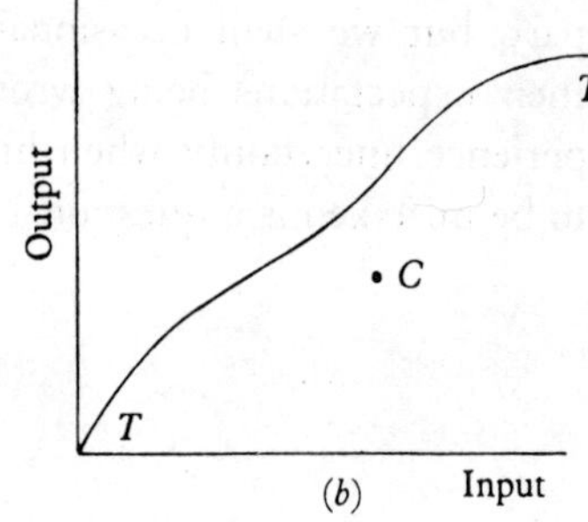

(*b*)

FIG. 1

productivities can be measured physically in terms of some numéraire good. Generally, however, we shall speak of the marginal 'rate' at which one good can be transformed into another —which is really just its 'opportunity cost' in terms of the good in question.

When production is so organized that society cannot get more of any one output without sacrificing other outputs or expending additional inputs, and cannot use less of any one input without using more of other inputs, or sacrificing outputs, we shall say that it is organized *optimally*. Thus, in the simple two-commodity worlds depicted in Figs. 1*a* and 1*b*, points like *C* are sub-optimal, whereas any point on TT is optimal. It need hardly be emphasized that there is nothing unique about the optimum in the engineering sense. There are an infinite number of points on TT.

The curve TT (or its multidimensional analogue in a world with more than two goods) we shall call the *social transformation function*. It describes society's potential productive powers. Just as a utility function in the theory of consumer behaviour describes the tastes of the consumer, so it describes the 'state of the arts' or the *technological knowledge* available to society. It tells us the maximum amount of any one output obtainable in a slice of time, given the amounts of the remaining outputs and of all the inputs; and it tells us the minimum amount of any one input required, in conjunction with fixed amounts of the remaining inputs, to produce a given collection of outputs.

When society is 'on' TT we shall often say that it is on its *production frontier*. This phrase will be used synonymously with 'optimal organization of production in the engineering sense'. Our task is to see how the social transformation function defining this frontier is related to the private production functions facing the individual firms in an economy. Before proceeding it is as well to note a minor difficulty.

From an engineering standpoint the distinction between inputs and outputs is simply that the former precede the latter in time. On this basis the smoke emitted from factory chimneys is an output. From a welfare standpoint, however, we presumably want to minimize its amount—it is an input in the sense of the value judgement propounded in our opening paragraph. Although examples of this sort can be multiplied, they need not worry us. The criteria for the optimal organization of production with which we shall chiefly be concerned are 'first-order' or 'marginal' ones. While sufficient for neither a maximum nor a minimum, they are necessary for both. We need not distinguish between the two at this stage of the argument. It should nevertheless be borne in mind that we really require a welfare classification of goods into inputs and outputs (or those which are not wanted and those which are) *before* pursuing our analysis at the engineering level.

THE PRIVATE TRANSFORMATION FUNCTIONS

When we try to construct a transformation function for society as a whole from those facing the individual firms comprising it, a fundamental difficulty confronts us. There is, from a welfare point of view, nothing special about the firms actually existing in an economy at a given moment of time. The firm is in no sense a 'natural unit'. Only the individual members of the economy can lay claim to that distinction. All are potential entrepreneurs. It seems, therefore, that the natural thing to do is to build up from the transformation functions of the men, rather than the firms, constituting an economy.

If we are interested in eventual empirical determination, this is extremely inconvenient. But it has its conceptual advantages. The ultimate repositories of technological knowledge in any society are the men comprising it, and it is just this knowledge which is effectively summarized in the form of a transformation function. In itself a firm possesses no knowledge. That which is available to it belongs to the men associated with it. Its production function is really built up in exactly the same way, and from the same basic ingredients, as society's.

Granted that the proper starting-point is the individual men, rather than the firms, there is a further difficulty. We do not assume that society is always on its production frontier. It is convenient, however, to assume that a man is always on his private production frontier. A psychologist might legitimately object that there is seldom anything 'optimal' about a man's organization of his activities, and that the transformation function connecting his observed inputs and outputs is not 'given' in any ultimate sense. But if there is to be some division of labour between the social sciences, economists have a right to take the private transformation functions as 'given', at least for a while. Indeed, most of modern welfare economics presupposes that they are 'given' in a very strict sense. We shall do the same until the end of the chapter, where we return to question the presupposition.

CERTAIN CONVENTIONS

Certain conventions are usually observed in defining private transformation functions, and therefore in the social one built out of them. It may save misunderstanding if we note them briefly.

(1) The classification of commodities must be sufficiently fine for two units of the same input (or output) to be perfect substitutes for each other. Physically identical goods relating to different slices of time are thus in general different commodities.

(2) The list of inputs and outputs whose amounts are explicitly included need not be restricted to economic ones. Such non-economic or exogenous factors as the temperature and humidity of the air can be included, but (in accordance with our distinction between general and economic welfare) we generally abstract from their presence by assuming them constant.

(3) All inputs and outputs must be measurable, either in physical units or in 'temporal' ones like man-hours. Any non-measurable factor must be subsumed in the *form* of the function: it cannot enter it explicitly as a variable.†

(4) 'Output' can be regarded as synonymous with 'production' or with 'production plus available inventories'. As long as 'input' is interpreted in the corresponding sense, no difficulty arises.

(5) A production function is defined with reference to a definite number of slices of time. We shall call the end of the period it embraces the time *horizon*.

(6) Installations of plant and machinery are to be regarded as inputs. Similarly, items of capital equipment extant when the horizon is attained are to be regarded as outputs. We shall call them *terminal* outputs.

(7) The depreciation of items of terminal capital equipment is assumed to occur in discrete steps. The mounting of each step

† Cf. Paul A. Samuelson, *Foundations of Economic Analysis* (Cambridge, Mass., 1947), pp. 84–5.

is regarded as the appearance of a new terminal output, and the disappearance of an old one.†

EXTERNAL EFFECTS

Let us suppose the diagrams of Fig. 1 to refer to a single person or firm. Then if the shape or position of *TT* depends in any way on the character or scale of operations of any other firm in the economy, we shall say that *external effects* are present. Stated more formally, they are present whenever a firm's production function depends in some way on the amounts of the inputs or outputs of another firm.

'External effects' embrace most of the external economies and diseconomies in production made famous by Marshall and Pigou. Two features of the definition should, however, be noted. Firstly, it is framed in terms of a firm (or, strictly, an individual man) rather than an 'industry'—which is rather a clumsy tool in welfare theory, however useful it may be in positive studies. Secondly, there is no mention of money cost or price. It is a purely technological definition. It therefore excludes those 'external economies which are internal to some other firm'—a phrase frequently encountered in the literature.‡ These occur when an expansion of output by one firm (or industry) makes it profitable for another to increase production, reap internal economies associated with large-scale operation, and lower (in monetary terms) average costs and prices. If this enables the original firm to buy its inputs more cheaply, its costs may fall too. But this is a market relationship, not a technological one. It is not an external effect in our sense.

The extent to which external effects exist in the world about us is an empirical question of the first importance. The only remark worth making at the theoretical level is that, apart from such

† Cf. 'The Classification of Commodities' in Chapter I. This procedure seems to be no more unsatisfactory than the alternative suggested by May: to include in the transformation function one variable for the stock of capital equipment involved in production, and a second measuring the extent of its use. Kenneth May, 'Structure of the Production Function of the Firm', *Econometrica*, vol. XVII (2) (1949), pp. 186–7.

‡ Cf. Jacob Viner, *Studies in the Theory of International Trade* (New York, 1937), pp. 479–82, and the literature there cited.

classic examples as 'smoke nuisance', the most marked effects seem likely to be those operating through *time*.† The skill of the labour force is the standard example: the efficiency of a man in his present work (and therefore the production function of the firm employing him) depends on how he has been employed in the past, and therefore on the input-output policies of the firms in which he has worked.

THE SOCIAL TRANSFORMATION FUNCTION

We are now in a position to see whether it is possible to build a social transformation function in a unique way out of the private ones. Dr Lange ‡ has expressed the view that the former is:

> a strong oversimplification of reality admissible only under special circumstances. . . . Only when the transformation functions of the individuals are all the same can they be combined in a unique way into a transformation function for society as a whole. Otherwise the conditions of transformation in society as a whole depend on how the transformation of commodities is distributed among individuals.

If Dr Lange means that the transformation function describing society's *actual* inputs and outputs is not unambiguously determined until we know 'how the transformation of commodities is distributed among individuals' (or, 'how resources are allocated', to use a more familiar phrase), he is perfectly correct. But if he means to refer to the function which defines society's production frontier, he would appear to be mistaken. For if we specify all the inputs, and all but one of the outputs, there is in general a determinate amount of the remaining output available to society. Its size, it is true, will usually depend on the way in which resources are allocated to the various firms, but its *maximum* size—that which lies on society's production frontier—is determined by a particular allocation, or set of allocations, and in fact itself implies one of those allocations. Now it is just this maximum size which we want the social transformation function to tell us. And it is

† This theme comes out strikingly in Maurice Dobb, *Soviet Economic Development since 1917* (London, 1948).

‡ Oscar Lange, 'Foundations of Welfare Economics', *Econometrica*, vol. x (1942), p. 224.

clear that by varying the inputs and other outputs the procedure can be repeated an indefinitely large number of times. Each time we have a maximum output (or minimum input) corresponding to given amounts of the remaining inputs and outputs. By combining these results a social transformation function can in general be built up.

The above argument, which could easily be made rigorous, is carried a step further in the appendix to this chapter, where the case of suitably smooth and continuous private transformation functions is treated mathematically. It is shown just how the social function can be constructed in a unique way—even when external effects are present.†

Some of the best known theorems of welfare economics emerge when we examine the characteristics of the distribution of the transformation of commodities (or allocation of resources) implied by the social transformation function. Let us consider varying amounts of two goods, X and Y; and let us keep all other inputs and outputs constant—not in each firm, but for society as a whole. Then we define the *marginal social rate of transformation* of Y into X as the rate at which Y is transformed into a marginal unit of X. Mathematically, it is simply $\partial Y/\partial X$.

Now imagine a marginal increment in the output of X by a particular firm (or person), the total output of X by the remaining firms being held constant. If society is *not* on its production frontier, the additional X can be obtained without varying Y, merely by shuffling inputs and outputs and moving them from one firm to another. But when it *is* on its production frontier, this shuffling process cannot with advantage be carried any further. More X can be secured only by expending (or sacrificing) more Y. If external effects are present, the additional Y expended by society as a whole may differ from the additional amount expended by the firm producing more X. That is to say: the marginal social

† When external effects are non-existent, there is a simple and well-known diagrammatic technique for deriving the social production function from two private ones. (Cf., e.g., J. R. Hicks, 'Foundations of Welfare Economics', *Economic Journal*, vol. XLIX (1939), esp. pp. 701–6.) The elaborate discussion of the text and appendix is needed to deal with situations in which they do exist.

rate may differ from the *marginal private rate of transformation*. But, whether the two differ or not, the assumption that society is on its production frontier implies one important result. It implies that the marginal social rate of transforming Y into X is the same in every firm where both are transformed. For, if it were larger in firm A than in firm B, it would be possible to transfer the production of X from A to B and obtain more than before from the same aggregate amount of Y—society would not have been on the frontier in the first instance. Moreover, in any firm where Y could be transformed into X, but is not, the marginal rate of transformation must be *larger* than it is in those firms where transformation does take place. That is: in those firms where Y is transformed into X, the amount of Y which would have to be sacrificed or expended (by society as a whole) to get a marginal unit of X must be *smaller* than in any firm where Y is not transformed into X.

These two basic marginal 'equivalences'—if I may use this term to cover both the equality and the inequality—have not been stated with complete accuracy. Clearly, there may be several different ways of using additional Y to get a marginal unit of X in a particular firm. However, if there are no external effects, so that all the additional Y is used in the firm in question, there will be a unique *minimum* amount if the firm operates on its private production frontier; and, if there are external effects, there will similarly be a unique minimum, arrived at by distributing the additional Y among the various firms in an optimal way (and perhaps † by reshuffling some of the other inputs and outputs).

† In the appendix to this chapter (see equations (12) and (13) and the accompanying discussion) the following theorem is proved. If society is on its production frontier, a reshuffling of inputs and outputs is required if, and only if, there are external effects associated with the transformation of Y. If there are not, the minimum amount of Y which has to be expended or sacrificed (in various parts of the economy) to save or produce a marginal unit of X in a particular firm is simply the amount expended in that firm plus the algebraic sum of the additional amounts expended in the other firms to keep their remaining inputs and outputs unchanged in the face of the production of the marginal unit of X in the original firm. (Naturally, the 'algebraic sum' is identically zero if there are no external effects associated with the transformation of X in the firm concerned.

When, however, there *are* external effects associated with the transformation of Y, the other firms may not be able 'to keep their remaining inputs and

It is obvious that the basic marginal equivalences must be stated in terms of these *minimum* marginal social rates of transformation, which tell us the *least* amounts of Y it is necessary to expend or sacrifice (in various parts of the economy) to save or produce marginal units of X in particular firms.

The first equivalence—the equality—can therefore be set out in the following general form: *if society is to be on its production frontier, it is necessary that the minimum marginal social rate of transformation between any two goods be the same in any two places where both are transformed.* The use of 'places' secures the optimal allocation of resources *within* firms as well as between them. The reader will have no difficulty in rephrasing the inequality in a similar way.

CORRECTIVE TAXES AND COMPETITION

The familiar result that perfect competition will, under certain circumstances, lead to an optimal allocation of resources is based on the satisfaction of the above marginal equivalences. Profit-maximizing entrepreneurs will attempt to equate their marginal private rates of transformation to given price ratios. Since uniform prices prevail on a competitive market, the marginal private rates will be the same in every firm. If, then, the marginal social rates are everywhere equal to the private ones, or if they are everywhere k-times them (where k is any constant), they too will be the same in every firm, and the first equivalence—the equality—will be satisfied. Moreover, by essentially similar reasoning it is straightforward to show that the correct *inequality* will be satisfied whenever a particular input or output is not transformed in a particular firm—the marginal private product being below price, or the marginal private cost being above it, for an 'incipient' use or production of the input or output in question.

What is the relationship between private and social rates of

outputs unchanged in the face of the production of the marginal unit of X in the original firm' if society is to remain on its production frontier. The correct course may be to add the additional Y where it yields most in the way of external economies, and least in the way of external diseconomies, reshuffling the other inputs and outputs in the process.

transformation (or costs and products) in fact likely to be? Clearly, they will always coincide in the absence of external effects. The rate at which a particular firm expends Y to get additional X will then be the same as that at which society expends it. But if there are external effects, there is a presumption that the two will diverge. To obtain an additional unit of X from a particular firm, more (or less) Y may be required in other firms if the total amounts of the remaining inputs and outputs are to be held constant for society as a whole. Indeed, unless the external effects fortuitously 'add up' to zero—the external economies just balancing the external diseconomies—a divergence will in general occur.

Under these circumstances perfect competition will not necessarily establish a uniform marginal social rate of transformation between any pair of goods. The classical remedy is to levy corrective taxes.† Ideally, they should discriminate between both goods and entrepreneurs. A particular entrepreneur, seeking maximum profits, will then try to equate his marginal private rate of transforming one good into another to the ratio of their prices, net of tax. By adjusting the tax, marginal private rates can, in principle, be made to diverge just enough to make marginal social rates coincide.

It is to be emphasized that the imposition of corrective taxes can only lead to the satisfaction of *necessary* conditions for the optimal organization of production. By themselves, they are *insufficient* to lead society to the production frontier. If, for instance, the number of firms is 'wrong', securing the satisfaction of the marginal equivalences may simply worsen the existing mal-allocation of resources. Now the number of firms is likely to be wrong whenever some of the correct number cannot earn positive profits. It is important to bear in mind that perfect competition satisfies the necessary marginal conditions for the attainment of the social production frontier simply because we assume that entrepreneurs seek maximum profits in a suitable environment (i.e. subject to fixed and uniform market prices, and appropriate

† A. C. Pigou, *The Economics of Welfare* (4th ed., London, 1932), Part II, Chaps. ix and xi. Cf. also R. F. Kahn, 'Some Notes on Ideal Output', *Economic Journal*, vol. XLV (1935), pp. 1–35.

corrective taxes). But there is no guarantee that the profits they maximize will prove sufficient to keep them in business. If they are not sufficient, further corrective devices, in the form of lump-sum subsidies, are required.

Even if the number of firms is optimal, there is the possibility of multiple equilibria.† Several positions inside the production frontier may well exist in which the marginal equivalences are satisfied. They will represent smaller amounts of all goods than other positions nearer the frontier where the marginal equivalences are not satisfied. Some form of corrective tax may be necessary to coax competitive entrepreneurs to the 'correct' equilibrium.

It is perhaps worth returning to lay special emphasis on the point that the marginal equivalences which perfect competition can be made to satisfy are only necessary for the attainment of the social production frontier, and by no means sufficient. It is instructive to consider what happens when (in the absence of external effects, and measuring outputs along the axes) a firm's production function is convex to the origin—i.e. when increasing (relative) marginal returns prevail over the whole range. If the firm faces fixed market prices for its outputs, it will find it profitable to concentrate on one of them. The correct marginal inequality will be satisfied for each of the outputs it does not produce—the marginal (opportunity) cost of an incipient unit will be above price (reckoned in terms of another good). But this does not mean that the social production frontier will necessarily be attained. It is quite easy to produce examples (*a*) where the firm should produce both outputs, and (*b*) where, while it should concentrate on one, it in fact concentrates on the wrong one.‡

The matter can be illustrated quite simply if we confine ourselves to a world (innocent of external effects) in which there are

† It is quite simple to show that when external effects do not exist and (outputs being measured along the axes) each firm's production function is concave to the origin—i.e. when diminishing (relative, marginal) returns prevail over the entire range—multiple equilibria are ruled out. The reader can experiment with the diagrammatic apparatus referred to on p. 20 n. to convince himself on this point. But when external effects exist and diminishing returns do not prevail universally, multiple equilibria may provide real difficulties.

‡ For a general discussion, see P. A. Samuelson, *Foundations of Economic Analysis* (Cambridge, Mass., 1947), pp. 231–5.

but two firms, each able to produce but two outputs (X and Y), and each endowed with a fixed supply of inputs which cannot be transferred from the one firm to the other. In the diagrams of Fig. 2 the first firm's production function ($T'T'$), and the axes to which it is referred, are drawn ordinarily; the second firm's are dotted. $T'T'$ is convex to its origin, O'; while $T''T''$ is concave to O'', whose position in relation to O' represents a maximal combination of X and Y. By sliding the dotted system in such a way that the two production functions are always in contact—either in a point of tangency or in a boundary point—O'' can be made to trace out the social production frontier.†

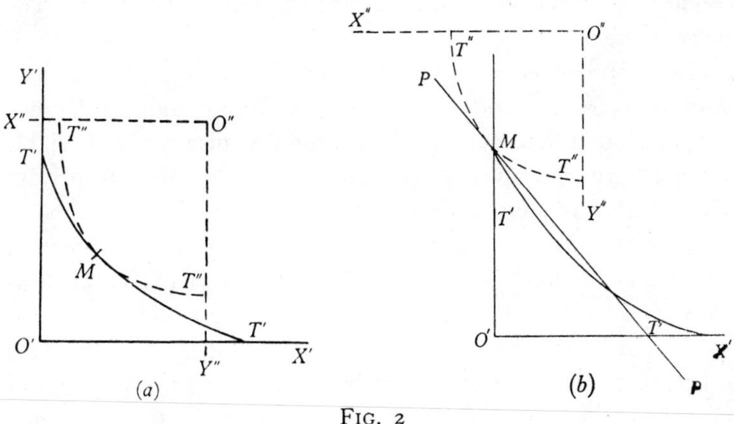

FIG. 2

Fig. 2*a* depicts the case where the first firm (which encounters increasing returns) should produce both X and Y—it should produce the combination represented by M. Yet, if we sketch in the contours indicating combinations of X and Y which yield the same profit (they will be parallel straight lines if the prices of X and Y are fixed), it is clear that M would be a point of *minimum* profit. To convert it into a point of maximum profit, so that a competitive extrepreneur would seek it out, it would be necessary to impose *ad valorem* taxes at a *variable* rate (so that the iso-profit lines are distorted into concave curves, the highest of which touches $T'T'$ in M).

† This is the well-known diagrammatic technique to which reference has been made (cf. p. 20 n.)

Fig. 2*b* depicts a case where the first firm should concentrate on the production of Y. But it will be observed that, at the price ratio necessary to make the second firm produce the optimal combination M (referred to O''), the first firm will find it profitable to concentrate on X instead. (In the diagram the price ratio in question is given by the slope of the iso-profit line, PP, passing through M.) To save the situation another tax is required.

If these additional corrective taxes are imposed, perfect competition can be made to satisfy the sufficient, as well as the necessary, conditions for the attainment of the social production frontier. But the taxes may be very complicated; and it may be a somewhat emaciated version of perfect competition which eventually emerges.

Those who advocate that state enterprises should play at competition in the real world often overlook these points. Sometimes they also forget that 'perfect' competition entails perfect foresight, which ensures the equality of an entrepreneur's estimated private rate of transformation with what the observing economist knows to be correct. It is occasionally argued that errors in estimation will at least 'tend to be eliminated', and that this is as much as one can ask for in the real world—that entrepreneurs will learn by experience and that those who do not will disappear. It seems to be implied that entrepreneurs bad at guessing in the past will prove bad at guessing in the future. This might be true in a static state, but it is a curious argument to apply to the world about us, where conditions in the future may differ appreciably from those obtaining in the past.†

THE DISTRIBUTION OF WEALTH

It is time to return to question the presupposition that the private transformation functions, as simple relations connecting inputs and outputs, are 'given' in any ultimate sense. It seems clear, for instance, that they depend upon the distribution of wealth—which is by no means 'given'. For the level of consumption a man

† The obverse of this remark is not irrelevant to the problem of finding managers for newly nationalized industries.

enjoys will in general have some effect on his efficiency in transforming one good into another.

Viewed from a more formal angle, the matter can be related to our classification of commodities. At first sight it might appear that physically identical units of output, produced in the same slice of time, were clearly perfect substitutes for one another. But if we look deeper we see that this is not necessarily so. In general, the distribution of outputs among final consumers will affect the efficiency of labour—which means that it will affect the classification of inputs. If we have already classified them as finely as we can, inputs of labour will be entering the production functions as 'hours' worked by particular men in particular jobs during particular slices of time. Now we have to recognize that a man's productivity may depend on what he has consumed in the past, and on what he consumes out of current output. When it does, we have no alternative but to distinguish (in both social and private transformation functions) between physically identical units of output going to different consumers.

If we take this complication into account, we can still construct a social transformation function.† It will, however, provide us with answers to a new sort of question. It will tell us the maximum amount of any one output it is possible to give to a particular man, given the amounts of the remaining inputs and outputs *and their distribution among final consumers*. It will, of course, still imply a determinate distribution, or set of distributions, of the *transformation* of commodities among the members of the community; but there seem to be no 'rules' for resource allocation as simple as those implied by the old social transformation function.

That the efficiency of men may bear some relation to the way in which they are fed is not a very profound observation. Yet most modern welfare theories implicitly ignore it. In Chapter IV, where we return to the matter, we shall refer to it by saying that the transformation functions may not be independent of the distribution of wealth.

† A brief comment on the formal procedure is contained in the appendix to this chapter.

APPENDIX TO CHAPTER II

Let us write x_i^α for the quantity of the ith good transformed by the αth person (or firm) in the relevant slice of time. We shall adopt the convention that i is an output when x_i^α is positive; an input when it is negative. We define X_i by

$$X_i = \sum_\alpha x_i^\alpha \qquad (i=1, ..., n) \qquad (1)$$

so that it is the community's net output of the ith good. Starting from ν private transformation functions of the form

$$t^\alpha(x_1^1, ..., x_n^1; ...; x_1^\nu, ..., x_n^\nu) = 0 \qquad (\alpha=1, ..., \nu) \qquad (2)$$

we seek a relation between the X_i of the form

$$T(X_1, ..., X_n) = 0 \qquad (3)$$

which will tell us the maximum value any one can take, given the values of the remaining ones. That is to say: we want to maximize, subject to the equations (2), each in turn of the X_i, holding on each occasion all the others constant. By performing the maximization process, a social transformation function can in general be built up. Note, however, that its representation is arbitrary to the extent that we can always replace T by $\phi(T)$ if $\phi(0) = 0$. A similar remark applies to the private functions.

If we are prepared to assume that the t^α have a certain degree of 'smoothness', defined by equation (15), we can proceed to construct T in a very simple way. Let us set up the Lagrangean expression

$$\sum_i \mu_i \sum_\alpha x_i^\alpha + \sum_\alpha \lambda^\alpha t^\alpha$$

where the ν λ's and all but one of the n μ's are undetermined multipliers. The remaining μ is set identically equal to unity; but to keep things symmetrical we shall not specify which particular X we are maximizing until a later stage of the argument.

The first-order conditions for a maximum are easily seen to be

$$\mu_i + \sum_\alpha \lambda^\alpha \frac{\partial t^\alpha}{\partial x^\beta} = 0. \qquad \begin{matrix}(\beta=1, ..., \nu)\\(i=1, ..., n)\end{matrix} \qquad (4)$$

We have in (1), (2) and (4) a set of $n+\nu+n\nu$ equations in the same number of unknowns: μ_i, λ^α and x_i^α. The distribution of commodities among firms is thus determined.

Taking total differentials of (2), multiplying by λ^α, and summing over the α, we have

$$\sum_i \sum_\beta \sum_\alpha \lambda^\alpha \frac{\partial t^\alpha}{\partial x_i^\beta} dx_i^\beta = 0,$$

which, in view of (4), may be written

$$\sum_{i}\sum_{\beta}\mu_i\, dx_i^\beta = 0,$$

or, recalling (1):

$$\sum_{i}\mu_i\, dX_i = 0. \tag{5}$$

Without loss of generality we can put $\mu_n \equiv 1$. Then, if the integrability conditions

$$\frac{\partial \mu_i}{\partial X_j} = \frac{\partial \mu_j}{\partial X_i} \qquad (i, j \neq n) \tag{6}$$

hold, the line integral

$$\int_c dX_n = -\int_c \sum_{i}^{n-1} \mu_i\, dX_i$$

will be independent of the path of integration. That is to say, there will exist a function

$$X_n = F(X_1, \ldots, X_{n-1})$$

such that

$$dF = -\sum_{i}^{n-1} \mu_i\, dX_i. \tag{7}$$

Writing

$$T(X_1, \ldots, X_n) = X_n - F = 0, \tag{8}$$

we have an expression for our social transformation function (3).

It will be convenient to postpone discussion of the second-order conditions until we have justified the integration.

PRIVATE AND SOCIAL RATES OF TRANSFORMATION

Note that we can express social rates of transformation in terms of the private ones. Thus, from (7) and (8):

$$\frac{\partial T/\partial X_i}{\partial T/\partial X_j} = \frac{\mu_i}{\mu_j} = \frac{\sum_{\alpha} \lambda^\alpha \frac{\partial t^\alpha}{\partial x_i^\beta}}{\sum_{\alpha} \lambda^\alpha \frac{\partial t^\alpha}{\partial x_j^\theta}} \qquad \begin{matrix} (i, j = 1, \ldots, n) \\ (\beta, \theta = 1, \ldots, \nu) \end{matrix} \tag{9}$$

recalling (4). Concentrating on a particular firm, say the θth, (9) yields:

$$\frac{\partial T/\partial X_i}{\partial T/\partial X_j} = \frac{\frac{\partial t^\theta}{\partial x_i^\theta} + \sum_{\alpha \neq \theta} \frac{\lambda^\alpha}{\lambda^\theta}\frac{\partial t^\alpha}{\partial x_i^\theta}}{\frac{\partial t^\theta}{\partial x_j^\theta} + \sum_{\alpha \neq \theta} \frac{\lambda^\alpha}{\lambda^\theta}\frac{\partial t^\alpha}{\partial x_j^\theta}}. \qquad (i, j = 1, \ldots, n) \tag{10}$$

The summations in (10) represent the external effects we encountered in the text.†

The most convenient way of interpreting (9) and (10) is by referring to equation (8). We have

$$-\frac{\partial T/\partial X_i}{\partial T/\partial X_j}=\left(\frac{\partial X_j}{\partial X_i}\right)_T=\frac{\mathrm{d}X_j}{\mathrm{d}x_i^\theta} \qquad (\theta=1, \ldots, \nu) \qquad (11)$$

recalling equations (1) and (5). The notation of partial derivatives is avoided in $\mathrm{d}X_j/\mathrm{d}x_i^\theta$, to emphasize that it is not taken 'on' any transformation function. It should, however, be noted that all the X_k are kept constant for $k \neq i, j$; and that the total variation in X_i occurs in the θth firm.

The expression $\mathrm{d}X_j/\mathrm{d}x_i^\theta$ is thus the marginal social rate of transformation of X_j into a marginal unit of X_i in the θth firm.‡ Letting θ take on its various values, equation (11) entails that, when society is on the frontier defined by its production function, the marginal social rate of transformation between any two goods must be the same wherever they are both transformed.

It is interesting to note that a simpler interpretation can be given to equations (9) and (10) if we make the (generally inadmissible) assumption that no external effects are associated with the transformation of a particular good, say the nth, anywhere in the economy. The equations (4) then reduce considerably for $i = n$, and we have

$$\frac{\lambda^\alpha}{\lambda^\theta}=\frac{\partial t^\theta/\partial x_n^\theta}{\partial t^\alpha/\partial x_n^\alpha}. \qquad (12)$$

Substituting (12) in (10), we have

$$\left(\frac{\partial X_n}{\partial X_i}\right)_T=\left(\frac{\partial x_n^\theta}{\partial x_i^\theta}\right)_{t^\theta}+\sum_{\alpha\neq\theta}\left(\frac{\partial x_n^\alpha}{\partial x_i^\theta}\right)_{t^\alpha}. \qquad (13)$$

If we regard the nth good as our numéraire, the left-hand side of (13) is the marginal social cost of X_i in terms of this numéraire. The whole equation may then be interpreted to mean: when society is on its production frontier and there are no external effects associated with the transformation of the numéraire, the marginal social cost of the ith good in any firm is its marginal private cost in that firm plus the algebraic sum of the additional amounts of the numéraire required by the other firms to keep their remaining inputs and outputs unchanged in

† Lange, 'Foundations of Welfare Economics', *Econometrica*, vol. x (1942), p. 228, equation (8), gives substantially the same result as that given by our equation (10), but omits the Lagrange multipliers.

‡ It is the *least* amount of X_j it is necessary to expend or sacrifice (in various parts of the economy) to save or produce a marginal unit of X_i in the θth firm.

the face of the expansion of output in the original firm. The interpretation breaks down when the assumption about the numéraire is relaxed because, if society is to remain on the frontier, the expansion of output will in general require a reshuffling of inputs and outputs among the firms.

INTEGRABILITY CONDITIONS

If we differentiate equations (1), (2) and (4) totally with respect to X_j, we obtain a system of $(n+\nu+n\nu)$ equations linear in the $(n+\nu+n\nu)$ variables $\partial\mu_i/\partial X_j$, $\partial\lambda^\alpha/\partial X_j$, $\partial x_i^\alpha/\partial X_j$. Writing δ_{ij} for the Kronecker delta, I for a column vector of unit matrices, and letting primes denote transposition, we have

$$\begin{bmatrix} 0 & 0 & I' \\ 0 & 0 & A' \\ I & A & B \end{bmatrix} \begin{bmatrix} \partial\mu/\partial X_j \\ \partial\lambda/\partial X_j \\ \partial x/\partial X_j \end{bmatrix} = \begin{bmatrix} \delta_{ij} \\ 0 \\ 0 \end{bmatrix}. \qquad (14)$$

The meaning of the matrices A and B is clear from the context.

Let us call the matrix of (14) D^*. Recalling the equations (4), it is easy to show that it is singular; but this is just the price we pay for symmetry. If, as before, we put $\mu_n \equiv 1$, we simply strike out the nth row and column in D^* to obtain a non-singular matrix D, whose determinant we shall call Δ. Then we have

$$\frac{\partial\mu_i}{\partial X_j} = \frac{\Delta_{ji}}{\Delta}; \text{ and } \frac{\partial\mu_j}{\partial X_i} = \frac{\Delta_{ij}}{\Delta},$$

where Δ_{ij} is the cofactor of the element in the ith row and j^{th} column of Δ. Now $\Delta_{ij} = \Delta_{ji}$ if $D = D'$, which clearly depends on whether $B = B'$. Writing this matrix out, its symmetry is seen to require

$$\frac{\partial^2 t^\theta}{\partial x_i^\alpha \partial x_j^\beta} = \frac{\partial^2 t^\theta}{\partial x_j^\beta \partial x_i^\alpha}. \qquad \begin{matrix} (\alpha, \beta, \theta = 1, \ldots, \nu) \\ (i, j = 1, \ldots, n) \end{matrix} \qquad (15)$$

Thus, if the private transformation functions are reasonably well-behaved, the integrability conditions (6) will be satisfied. It is worth noting, however, that (15) will not in general be satisfied on the boundaries of the domains in which the private functions are defined. It is clear that there are such boundaries, for if in any transformation function we put all inputs equal to zero, and abstracted from inventories, we could not have any output positive.

This remark may be relevant when increasing returns prevail and a firm operates on the boundary of its production function's domain of definition. The method we have used to form the social transformation function cannot then be justified without a rather lengthy argument. Note that, if we are not interested in actually forming the social function we can give a limited interpretation to equation (5), which places fewer restrictions on the private production functions—they need only be differentiable once. Referring to equation (4), we can obtain a result analogous to equation (9). But the marginal social rates of substitution involved cannot without further argument be identified with the slope of a social transformation function; and, it should be noted, (5) may itself break down on the boundary of a domain.

SECOND-ORDER CONDITIONS

So far we have not mentioned the second-order conditions which ensure that X_n is at a regular maximum, rather than a minimum or a stationary value. They are equivalent to D being the matrix of a quadratic form, negative definite under constraint. Since the choice of n is arbitrary, this implies similar restrictions on the matrices of the first n principal cofactors of the determinant of D^*.

Certain restrictions on the inverse of D are also implied; and these enable us to show that, in the absence of external effects, T must be concave (to the origin) if all the t^α are concave too—i.e. that society will encounter diminishing returns if all the individuals comprising it do. Although this leads to some results of great elegance, there is from an economic standpoint little purpose in pursuing them.

THE DISTRIBUTION OF WEALTH

Hitherto our object has been to derive a social T of the form given by (3) from the private t's given by (2). When, however, the private functions depend upon the distribution of wealth, they must be written in the form

$$t^\theta(x; z) = 0 \qquad (\theta = 1, \ldots, \nu)$$

where x and z are row vectors whose elements are x_i^α and z_j^β $(i, j = 1, \ldots, n;$ $\alpha, \beta = 1, \ldots, \nu)$. If z_j^β is positive it represents the consumption of the jth good by the βth man; if negative, the amount of the jth productive service rendered by him. The z's, in short, enter into the *utility functions* of the members of the community as well as into their transformation functions. The x's have their previous meanings.

Proceeding as before, we can build a social transformation function of the form

$$T^{**}(x; z) = 0.$$

But if we assume that the total consumption of any good is equal to its net output, we have n relations connecting the elements of x and z

$$\sum_\alpha x_i^\alpha = \sum_\alpha z_i^\alpha \qquad (i = 1, \ldots, n)$$

and so we can rewrite $T^{**}(x; z)$ in the form $T^*(z)$. This is the social transformation function we require.

CHAPTER III

TASTES

The last chapter has given a fairly complete survey of what Dr Myint, harking back to the classical labour theory of value, has called welfare analysis at the physical level, which 'provisionally assumes that quantities of satisfaction are proportionate to quantities of physical products'.† The present chapter lays the foundations for welfare analysis at the *subjective level*, by inquiring into the meaning we can attach to phrases like 'quantities of satisfaction' or 'utility'.

UTILITY AND CHOICE

We have already defined a man's welfare map to be identical with his preference map, which indicates how he would choose between different situations if he were given the opportunity for choice. Let it be said at once that most people would probably want to regard this as a definition of welfare *ex ante*, rather than welfare *ex post*; and that most people probably feel that the latter is the more significant concept. It is, however, very hard to think of a way of defining welfare *ex post*. We could, of course, simply assume that the observing economist knew what it was, or that we had a lie-detector and could question people to find out if they were better off yesterday than the day before. But neither of these assumptions is very helpful, and if we want to make any progress we shall have to be content with welfare *ex ante*. To pretend that we can distinguish between the two concepts in practice, and for people other than ourselves, leads very rapidly to a paternalist approach—not only to group welfare, but to individual welfare itself.

Having defined preference in terms of conjectural choices, we are left with a crude behaviourist concept which is suitable for formal analysis, but awkward in exposition. For expository purposes

† Hla Myint, *Theories of Welfare Economics* (London, 1948), p. 230.

it is extremely convenient to be able to talk of 'indifference', or of a person being 'just as well off in A as in B'. Just how these expressions should be defined involves philosophical questions of some nicety, which I shall disregard. It seems clear, however, that 'indifference' cannot be defined in behaviourist terms.† I shall therefore simply postulate that it is possible to represent a man's hypothetical choices by a function, u, such that A is chosen in preference to B if, and only if, $u(A) > u(B)$; and shall call the contours of this function 'indifference surfaces'. I shall say that A and B represent 'equal levels of well-being' if, and only if, they lie on the same contour—i.e. if $u(A) = u(B)$.

The function describing a man's hypothetical choices can be called his *utility* function. It should be emphasized that it *describes* choices, and in no way seeks to *explain* them. It represents *tastes* in the same way as a transformation function represents 'the state of the arts'. Its name is, for historical reasons, rather unfortunate. It tempts people to ask if 'utility' is measurable. If we spoke instead of a 'hypothetical choice function', few would wonder if 'hypothetical choice' were measurable. To this matter a separate section is devoted. For the moment it is important to know just what is implied by the postulate that a utility function exists.

Assuming the existence of a utility function amounts to assuming away the 'problem of integrability', which has been discussed by mathematical economists since the days of Irving Fisher and Pareto.‡ Put briefly, and somewhat loosely, integrability entails a certain degree of consistency in the making of choices. Professor Houthakker§ has recently given a definitive treatment of the case where a man's demand functions are single-valued and continuously differentiable with respect to prices and income. He shows that the necessary and sufficient condition for integrability

† Cf. I. M. D. Little, 'The Theory of Consumer's Behaviour—a Comment', *Oxford Economic Papers*, vol. II, no. 1 (1950), pp. 132–5, and the preceding discussion in the same journal; also: W. E. Armstrong, 'The Determinateness of the Utility Function', *Economic Journal*, vol. XLIX (1939).

‡ See N. Georgescue-Roegen, 'The Pure Theory of Consumer's Behavior', *Quarterly Journal of Economics*, vol. L (1935–6), pp. 545–93.

§ H. S. Houthakker, 'Revealed Preference and the Utility Function', *Economica*, vol. XVII (1950), pp. 159–74.

is, roughly, the following: If A is preferred to B, B to C, C to...Y, and Y to Z, then Z must not be preferred to A.

It will be seen that very little is really implied by the assumption that a utility function exists—and I suspect (although this is still an unsolved problem) that relaxing the restrictions on the demand functions would not alter the position greatly. In any event, the utility function is primarily an expository device enabling us to talk about indifference curves without abandoning a behaviourist approach to welfare. It in no way taints our analysis with hedonism. If the limited degree of consistency it entails were to be rejected on empirical grounds, it would simply strengthen some of the criticisms of welfare theory we shall develop with its aid.

THE IRRELEVANCE OF MEASURABILITY

Assuming the existence of a utility function does not entail assuming the existence of any such thing or quantity as 'utility' or 'satisfaction'. Our definition of individual welfare still runs in terms of conjectural choices. But when economists were interested in explaining choices, and not just in describing them, it seemed natural to suppose that a man would choose A rather than B if he anticipated greater satisfaction, or utility, from the former. Then 'preference' meant something more than 'conjectural choice'. The problem of the 'measurability' of utility, or the 'quantitative variability of preference', was relevant. It made sense to ask if you could compare one *change* in utility with another; and, if you could, the resulting demonstration that utility was measurable (once an origin and a scale had been selected) was very much to the point.†

When however, we do not seek an explanation for choices (and classical utility theory is not really an 'explanation' worth seeking —it is little more than tautology), to say that 'the utility of A is

† See Oscar Lange, 'The Determinateness of the Utility Function', *Review of Economic Studies*, vol. I (1934), pp. 218–25, which should be read in conjunction with P. A. Samuelson, 'The Numerical Representation of Ordered Classifications and the Concept of Utility', *Review of Economic Studies*, vol. VI (1938–9), pp. 65 ff. Note that the whole problem is irrelevant if we confine ourselves to observable behaviour, as we cannot ask how a man would choose between *changes* in situations—choices between situations themselves are the only conceivable ones.

greater than the utility of B' is just a *way of saying* that A would be chosen. Whether or not utility is measurable—and whether or not it exists—is irrelevant. If we have $u(A) > u(B)$, we can always replace u by an arbitrary transform of itself, $\phi(u)$, as long as ϕ increases when u increases—for then $\phi(A) > \phi(B)$ is entailed. The choice will still fall on A. But this property of the representation of u leads naturally to the expression that 'utility is measurable up to a monotone transformation'—which is unfortunate, as it quite unnecessarily suggests that utility is some thing or quantity which exists. 'Utility is an *ordinal* quantity' gives the same unnecessary impression.

All this is commonplace and would not be worth mentioning had not two views recently won ground. The first is that Professors von Neumann and Morgenstern have discovered a way of measuring utility up to a linear transformation—i.e. of measuring it (like time or temperature) from an arbitrary origin on an arbitrary scale. And the second is that the whole problem has something to do with welfare economics. Let us examine these views in turn.

In the *Theory of Games* † Professors von Neumann and Morgenstern base their treatment on the hypothesis that a man faced by choices involving risk will seek to maximize the mathematical expectation (or actuarial value) of his 'utility'. Two premisses are implicit in this hypothesis: that a man maximizes the mathematical expectation, rather than some other characteristic expression (such as one involving skewness), of a set of quantities when confronted with choices involving risk; and that these quantities can justifiably be identified with the utility of classical economic analysis. Neither premiss is particularly secure. The authors are aware that the first excludes the possibility of there being any specific 'utility' or 'disutility' attached to gambling or risk-taking, as such. It would seem better, therefore, to call the von Neumann-Morgenstern 'utility' *nutility*, and to say that

† John von Neumann and Oskar Morgenstern, *Theory of Games and Economic Behavior* (Princeton, 1944), esp. pp. 15–31 and appendix to second edition. This and the next paragraph are taken with minor changes from a footnote to p. 87 of my article: 'Mr Harrod on Hump Saving', *Economica*, vol. XVII (1950), pp. 81–90.

there is no nutility attached to gambling or risk-bearing—for to use 'utility' in such a way that none can attach to these activities is to depart rather far from the traditional usage.

This is but one example of a difficulty frequently encountered when the axiomatic approach is employed (and it is very extensively employed in the *Theory of Games*). The difficulty arises because, when one has axiomatized a concept, it is often by no means easy to find the intuitive counterpart of the concept which satisfies one's axioms. Thus, to identify the nutility measured by the von Neumann-Morgenstern method with the utility of classical analysis, let alone with welfare in the sense in which we have defined it, is to make a very big jump.

The idea that the measurability of utility has something to do with welfare economics dies very hard.† It probably springs from the belief that interpersonal comparisons of well-being require measurable well-being for any one person,‡ but Professor Bergson showed this to be false in 1938.§ We can number men's indifference curves and formalize our ethical judgements regarding the way in which their various levels of indifference contribute to social welfare without mentioning utility or its measurement. The Bergson welfare function, $W(u^1, \ldots, u^\nu)$, is defined for a particular choice of the ordinal utility indicators $(u^1, \ldots, u^\nu)$. If we want to replace any one of them by an arbitrary transform of itself, we simply redefine W. And if the u's did have cardinal significance it would in no way alter the fact that we have to make ethical judgements to compare them, or evaluate their contribution to social welfare.

Given a definite set of individual ordinal utility indicators, the measurability of W itself is an open question. If our ethical beliefs are such that we can attribute some clear meaning to sentences like

† Cf. D. H. Robertson, 'On Sticking to One's Last', *Economic Journal*, vol. LIX (1949), pp. 505 ff.; *idem*, 'A Revolutionist's Handbook', *Quarterly Journal of Economics*, vol. LXIV (1950), esp. pp. 6–7.

‡ Cf. Professor Sir Dennis Robertson's remark, *ibid*. 'But I do not myself see how one can make such judgements without the aid of prior knowledge of a law of diminishing marginal utility of real income in the case of the individual.' (Diminishing marginal utility entails measurability up to a linear transformation; cf. Lange, *art. cit.*)

§ Abram Bergson (Burk), 'A Reformulation of Certain Aspects of Welfare Economics', *Quarterly Journal of Economics*, vol. LII (1938), pp. 310–34.

'social welfare is twice as great in A as in B', then W has cardinal significance. But for the problems with which we shall be dealing it will be sufficient to know that social welfare is greater in A—the question 'How much greater?' will not concern us. It should be noted, however, that it is quite possible for W to have cardinal significance even if the individual utilities have not.

The essentials of the matter can be stated in four propositions: (i) Since we are interested in how a man would choose if he were given the opportunity for choice, the measurability of utility is irrelevant as long as the utility function does describe his choices. (ii) 'Utility', 'satisfaction' or 'individual welfare' need not necessarily exist. To say that it is higher in one situation than another is just a way of saying how the man concerned would choose. (iii) Exactly the same ethical judgements are required to pass from individual choices to social welfare whether or not such a thing or quantity as utility exists, whether or not it is measurable. (iv) The nature of those ethical judgements, and nothing else, determines the measurability of social welfare.

While there is no doubt that the measurability of individual welfare or utility is wholly irrelevant to the problems we shall be discussing, it may not be without interest to draw attention to a method of 'proving' its measurability which has a fair degree of plausibility, and which I can commend to all would-be utilitarians. In a recent survey † Professor Bergson has suggested that an individual man may find his 'total utility' affected by the standards of living enjoyed by other men, even if his choices for items of personal consumption are unaffected. Now, although Professor Bergson does not mention it, it can be shown that, if this is the case over a finite range, the man's 'total utility' must be measurable up to a linear transformation.

The first point to get clear is just what it means to say that utility is affected by the standards of living (or consumption-patterns) of others, even if choices for items of personal consump-

† H. S. Ellis (ed.), *A Survey of Contemporary Economics* (Philadelphia, 1948), p. 419 n. It should perhaps be remarked that Professor Bergson's suggestion runs in terms of households rather than individual men.

tion are unaffected. It means, firstly, that the man's indifference map (for items of personal consumption) is quite independent of the consumption of others; but that, *if he were allowed to choose the consumption patterns of others for them*, he would have definite preferences on the matter. Mathematically, we can express it $U_{xy} \equiv 0$, but U_x and $U_y \neq 0$, where we write x for the man's own consumption, y for that of others, and $U(x, y)$ for his 'total utility'. For the first of these properties to be invariant under a transformation of the form $\phi(U)$, we must have $\phi_{xy} \equiv 0$. But

$$\phi_{xy} = \phi'(U)U_{xy} + \phi''(U)U_xU_y$$

which is in general zero only if $\phi''(U)$ is zero. That is to say:

$$\phi(U) = aU + b$$

and 'total utility' is measurable once we have chosen the scale, a, and the origin, b.

What we have in effect assumed is that the utility of personal consumption and the utility derived from the external economies and diseconomies of (at least one item of) another's consumption are *independent* of each other—and it is well known that an assumption of independence always entails measurability.† Whether or not it is a plausible assumption is of course a subject for empirical investigation. But, if it is plausible, it implies that utility can be regarded as a quantity which exists, and not just as a word describing observable behaviour.

For my part, I think the way we have introduced the assumption of independence does make it seem quite plausible. A perfectly 'ordinary' man may be found whose preferences display the required characteristic. Now (and this is where sophistry enters the argument) if utility is measurable for him, why should we not assume that it is measurable for other 'ordinary' men too, even if their preferences do not display the particular characteristic which would enable us to be sure that it is? (The fact that they

† Cf. P. A. Samuelson, *Foundations of Economic Analysis* (Cambridge, Mass., 1947), pp. 174 ff. I think Samuelson overstates the case against independence. Note that the very weak assumption that *one* pair of goods (x and y) are independent (in the sense $U_{xy} \equiv 0$) is sufficient for measurability. Samuelson is inclined to assume universal independence, which is easy to criticize.

do not display the characteristic does not disprove measurability, it merely fails to indicate it.) Here I leave the question for the reader to answer, simply reminding him that the whole matter is largely irrelevant as far as welfare theory is concerned.

A final implication of our method of approach should be noted. Until someone suggests a way in which an observable choice can be made between 'n units of present utility and one unit of utility tomorrow', we cannot speak of *time-preference*. We can, of course, speak of an 'intertemporal rate of substitution'—the additional amount of a good a man must get today to compensate for a unit less tomorrow—but that is something quite different. I do not think that the scrapping of time-preference is to be mourned. Indeed, being doubtful of its existence† in the first place, I do not think it will even be missed.

THE UTILITY FUNCTION: CERTAIN CONVENTIONS

Having emphasized as strongly as possible that we are not interested in the existence, let alone the measurability, of 'utility', 'satisfaction' or 'individual welfare', let us proceed to note certain conventions we shall observe in using a utility function to describe conjectural choices. The analogies with those observed in defining a transformation function will be obvious.

(1) The classification of commodities must be sufficiently fine for two units of the same good (in which term we include the productive services a man renders) to be perfect substitutes for each other in the opinion of the man concerned. Physically identical goods purchased in different slices of time are thus in general different commodities. The 'same' productive service rendered in different firms is 'the same' only if the man is indifferent as to the firm in which he works.

(2) All variables entering u explicitly must be capable of measurement in physical units or 'temporal' ones like 'hours worked'. In accordance with our distinction between general

† I cannot see that the question 'How much present utility would you give up for an extra unit of utility tomorrow?' is anything but utterly meaningless. Without a lie-detector there is no obvious way of checking whatever answer is given—be it zero or infinite.

and economic welfare, we abstract from non-economic variables (whether measurable or not) by assuming them constant.

(3) Leisure does not enter explicitly. If we know the length of the relevant slice of time and the amounts of productive services rendered during that slice, it is the residue.

(4) Since we are abstracting from uncertainty, u is assumed to be independent of prices, forms of market organization, etc.

(5) We shall *not* assume u to be independent of the consumption (or purchases) of other men. A separate section is devoted to these 'external effects' in consumption.

(6) The remaining variables entering u are of two types. Firstly, there are the man's own purchases of goods (and sales of productive services). The emphasis is on *purchase*, rather than consumption. A significant difference is likely to arise only in connection with durable consumers' goods. We shall confine ourselves to the welfare aspects of their production and purchase. The rates at which any one of their purchasers consumes them are, so to speak, his own affair. A difficulty may arise in connection with external effects: a man's choices may sometimes be affected by the consumption, rather than the purchases, of others. From this, however, we shall abstract; and we shall henceforth use 'purchase' and 'consumption' synonymously.

(7) The second of the two remaining types of variable comprises *collective* goods, which a man cannot (or does not) purchase for himself. Public parks, police protection and other standard examples spring to mind. For our purposes it is convenient to include *advertising* in this category. It is measurable (in terms of resources expended on it), it is seldom consciously purchased, and it affects choices. There is thus no case for ignoring it.

(8) The utility function is drawn up with reference to a definite number of slices of time. The end of the period it embraces we shall call its *horizon*. It may precede the death of the man concerned. 'Latent wants' for new commodities not invented at the beginning of the period are included †—the observing economist

† For a different view, see Maurice Dobb, *Soviet Economic Development since 1917* (London, 1948), p. 18 n.

knows how a man would choose (if given the opportunity for choice) in the face of any conceivable set of circumstances.

(9) It is usually assumed that, if we confine attention to those goods a man purchases for himself, indifference curves are convex to the origin. We shall, in general, *not* make this assumption. Its conventional basis is that, if a consumer can trade at fixed market prices, and ends up in equilibrium with a definite collection of goods, his indifference surfaces must be convex to his budget plane (and thus to the origin) in the neighbourhood of the equilibrium point.† This 'stability condition' is then assumed to obtain universally—i.e. every point is assumed to be a potential equilibrium point. There seems to be no particular reason why we should

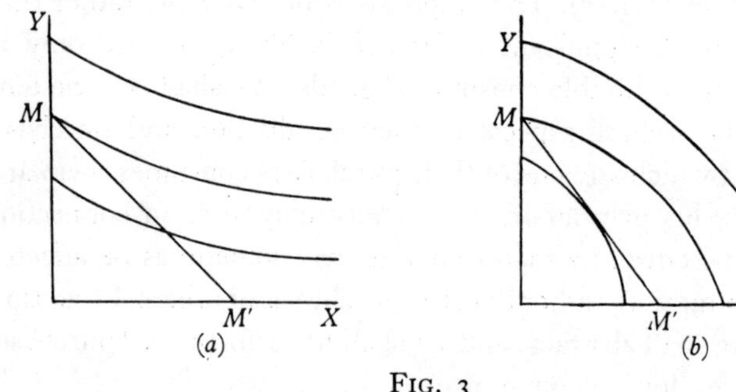

FIG. 3

make this assumption in welfare theory (in positive economics, where we can test against the facts the conclusions to which it leads, it is a legitimate simplification). Moreover, the argument does not apply when external effects are present, or when a man purchases zero amounts of some goods.

When will a man purchase zero amounts of some goods? Consider for simplicity the two-dimensional case, where the two goods are X and Y. A man may purchase no X in four circumstances: (i) when there are indivisibilities (from which we abstract until Chapter VII); (ii) when he has no preference for X, or positively dislikes it; (iii) when his indifference curves, although convex to the origin, intersect the Y-axis; and (iv) when his

† Cf. J. R. Hicks, *Value and Capital* (Oxford, 1939), pp. 21 ff.

indifference curves are not convex to the origin. Figs. 3*a* and 3*b* depict (iii) and (iv). MM' is the budget line, and M (representing zero purchase of X) the point where the highest indifference curve is attained. In view of the observed fact that most people do consume some goods in zero amounts. there does not seem to be any ground for excluding case (iv). Unless the contrary is stated, therefore, we shall not assume convex preference fields.

EXTERNAL EFFECTS

External effects exist in consumption whenever the shape or position of a man's indifference curves depends on the consumption of other men. In the main, there has been a tendency for professional economists—with notable exceptions†—to ignore them. Nothing very profound is required to cast doubt on the validity of such a procedure. It is enough to recall the examples of 'top-hats and diamonds' given by Pigou‡ at the turn of the century; to think of the emphasis Veblen§ laid on envy and emulation as factors determining demand; to observe the tide of fashion in women's clothing; or to imagine what would happen to any one man's desire for a telephone || if those of all his friends were permanently disconnected.

Note that these external effects are, broadly, of two kinds. Telephones are the standard example of goods giving external economies; 'ostentatious diamonds' of those giving diseconomies. But it is probable that these Pigovian and Veblenesque elements, striking though they may be, are of small importance when compared with the whole social process of taste formation—with that mysterious complex of effects which operates through *time*. Not

† Apart from the writers mentioned below, see James S. Duesenberry, *Income, Saving and the Theory of Consumer Behavior* (Cambridge, Mass., 1949); William J. Baumol, *The Theory of Welfare and Control* (L.S.E. Ph.D. dissertation, 1948; subsequently published as *Welfare Economics and the Theory of the State*, (London, 1952)); G. Tintner, 'A Note on Welfare Economics', *Econometrica*, vol. XIV (1946), pp. 69–78; Lionel Robbins, *The Economic Problem in Peace and War* (London, 1947), esp. pp. 18 ff.; and the many writings of J. M. Clark and F. H. Knight.

‡ A. C. Pigou, 'Some Remarks on Utility', *Economic Journal*, vol. XIII (1903), p. 62.

§ T. Veblen, *The Place of Science in Modern Civilization* (New York, 1919).

|| R. W. Souter, *Prolegomena to Relativity Economics* (New York, 1933), pp. 50 ff.

all the effects operating through time are external, of course. A man's choices are affected by his *own* history as well as by the consumption-patterns which have evolved in the society in which he lives. But the importance of the latter is too obvious to be ignored. And if our own observation were insufficient at this point, it would only be necessary to turn to the rich variety of examples gathered by social anthropologists—especially by those who have studied the impact of western civilization on primitive ways of life.† Little room is left for doubt about the extent to which tastes (and, naturally, especially those of the young) are moulded by social forces.

We need hardly go as far afield as anthropology. Marshall himself emphasized the *conventional* character, at any given time, of certain of the 'necessaries of life', and the continuous 'interaction of wants and activities'.‡ He would probably have agreed with Veblen that 'invention is the mother of necessity'—but here the weight of his authority is perhaps superfluous: the reader can consult any advertising agent.

Custom and fashion, the cultural conditioning of our childhood years—these determine choices quite as much as the deeper biological forces rooted in our natures, and which alone have any degree of permanence during our lives.§ Moreover, it must not be thought that it is only preference for consumers' goods which is subject to these influences. A man's choice of a job not infrequently depends on what other men (or types of men) choose similar work—or different work in the same factory or office.‖ There can be little doubt that the status of the professions is to a large extent the product of external effects.

Enough has probably been said to emphasize the importance of external effects. It is perhaps as well to end with a reminder that,

† Cf. I. Schapera, *Married Life in an African Tribe* (London, 1940); *idem* (ed.), *Western Civilization and the Natives of South Africa* (London, 1934); Ruth Benedict, *Patterns of Culture* (New York, 1935).

‡ A. Marshall, *Principles* (8th ed., 1920), pp. 67–70 and 88–90.

§ Cf. Bronislaw Malinowski, *A Scientific Theory of Culture* (Chapel Hill, N.C., 1944).

‖ It is unnecessary to go all the way with Elton Mayo to agree with this. See his *The Human Problems of an Industrial Civilization* (New York, 1933)

however important they may be, the ordinary 'internal' effects do still exist.

COMMUNITY INDIFFERENCE: THE SCITOVSKY FRONTIER

In the last chapter we started off from the private production frontiers of the members of the community and showed how they determined a unique social production frontier. In exactly the same way we can pass from individual tastes to 'social tastes'. A difficulty does, however, arise. Whereas each man has but one transformation curve, he has a whole set of indifference curves. Which one should we select as a basis for the community indifference curve?

We shall see that this question cannot be answered without recourse to ethical judgements. We shall therefore postpone it for a while. Consider for the moment an *arbitrary* selection of individual indifference curves, one for each member of the community. To focus attention on the ones selected, let us call them the *prescribed* curves. Now (adopting the convention that rendering productive services is consuming negative amounts of goods) let us assume that we have given us definite amounts of all goods but one. Then we ask: What is the *minimum* amount of the remaining good which will suffice to place each man on his prescribed indifference curve? The answer will give us a point on the *Scitovsky community indifference curve* † corresponding to the prescribed set of individual curves. By varying the amounts of the other goods, and repeating the procedure, the complete Scitovsky curve (or, strictly, multidimensional surface) can in general be built up.

Fig. 4 depicts the case where there are varying amounts of two goods, X and Y, the amounts of the others being held constant—not for each man, but for society as a whole. (In the figure both X and Y are 'positive goods', but productive services could just as easily have been considered.) SS is the Scitovsky curve. Given any amount of either X or Y, it tells us the minimum

† T. de Scitovsky, 'A Reconsideration of the Theory of Tariffs', *Review of Economic Studies*, vol. IX (2) (1941–2), pp. 89–110. (Reprinted in *Readings in the Theory of International Trade* (Philadelphia, 1949).)

amount of the other required to keep each member of the community on his prescribed indifference curve. Now assume that, although each member of the community is still at his prescribed level of well-being, we have the collection of goods represented by C. Clearly, X and Y cannot have been distributed among the members of the community in an optimal fashion. For we can achieve the same result (in terms of levels of individual well-being) by moving to a point like P, where the amounts of both X and Y are smaller. The situation is precisely analogous with that depicted in Fig. 1, where C represented a point inside the social production frontier. Indeed, it is helpful to refer to SS as the *Scitovsky frontier*; and, as before, we can find a set of conditions which must be fulfilled if society is to be on its frontier.

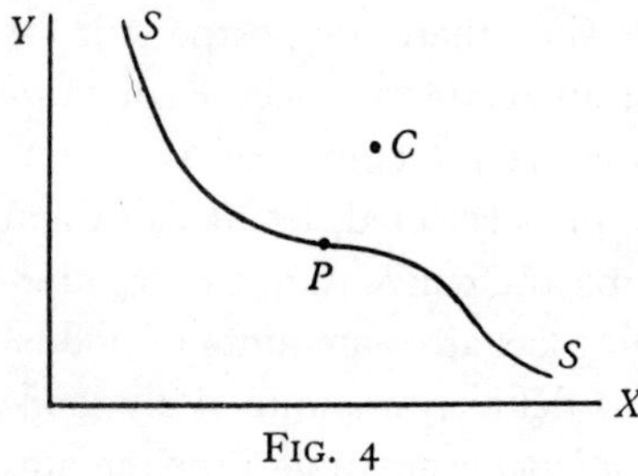

FIG. 4

Let us first define a familiar term. The *marginal social rate of substitution* of X for Y is the amount of Y taken away to compensate for the gain of a marginal unit of X, each man being kept on his prescribed indifference curve. As before, the amounts of all other goods are kept constant for society as a whole. This term has become established, but (in view of the association of 'substitution' and 'substitutability' with the theory of production) it will sometimes be convenient to speak of the *marginal social rate of indifference* between two goods.

Imagine a marginal decrement in the amount of X consumed by a particular man—the total amount of X consumed by other men being held constant. How much Y is required to maintain the prescribed levels of individual well-being? If society is not on the Scitovsky frontier, no additional Y may be required. A mere reshuffling of goods may be sufficient. But if it is on the frontier, more Y is in general necessary. If external effects are absent, all of it will go to the man suffering the loss of X. If external effects exist, however, some may have to be given to (or taken away from) other men if they are to be kept on their prescribed indifference curves. That is to say, the *marginal private rate of substitution* (the amount of Y given to the original man to compensate for his loss of X) may differ from the marginal social rate. But, whether the two differ or not, the fact that society is on the Scitovsky frontier implies results which are simple analogues of the necessary conditions for the optimal organization of production. The method of reasoning being identical in the two cases, we need do no more than state them:

(i) If society is to be on the Scitovsky frontier, the marginal social rate of substitution between any two goods must be the same in the case of each man who consumes both.

(ii) If a man consumes one, but not both, of the goods, the rate must be less than it is for those men who do consume them both.

(iii) The rates of substitution involved in (i) and (ii) must be *maximum* ones—not in any absolute sense, but with respect to changes in the distribution of a fixed quantity of goods.

CORRECTIVE TAXES AND COMPETITION

It is well known that if consumers are allowed to trade at fixed prices on a perfect market (which implies that they have perfect knowledge), and if there are no external effects, the above conditions will be satisfied. Private and social rates of indifference will coincide. A consumer, seeking maximum utility, will come into equilibrium with his budget line just touching an indifference curve (provided that his indifference curves are not concave to the origin). That is to say, he will equate his marginal private rate of indifference between any pair of goods to the given price ratio. Since the latter is uniform throughout the market, so is the former —and hence the marginal social rate—wherever both goods are purchased. Moreover, he will not purchase a good if its price (in terms of some numéraire) exceeds its marginal private rate of substitution for the numéraire—cf. Fig. 3*a*.

If external effects are present, and private rates of indifference diverge from the social rates (i.e. if external economies and diseconomies do not fortuitously balance), all will still be well if they are everywhere k-times the latter—k being any constant. Failing this, *ad valorem* corrective taxes can be imposed, discriminating between goods and between consumers. They can cause private rates to differ just enough for the social rates to coincide. As in production, the necessary conditions for the attainment of the frontier will be fulfilled. As in production, that does not necessarily mean that the frontier will actually be attained.†

All this is familiar and obvious. What requires emphasis is that the Scitovsky frontier is defined with reference to prescribed levels of well-being for each member of the community. Lump-sum taxes and bounties may have to be imposed to secure the fulfilment of the prescription. Moreover, the sizes of these taxes, and of the *ad valorem* ones, will naturally depend on the particular set of individual indifference curves prescribed—on the ethical judgements made. No such ethical content is possessed by the *ad valorem* taxes needed to correct production. The former involve interpersonal comparisons of well-being: the latter do not.

To sum up: the operation of a perfect market, corrected by suitable lump-sum and *ad valorem* taxes, could lead society to the Scitovsky frontier. That is to say, it could secure the most 'economical' distribution of a given collection of goods—in the sense that it would not be possible to attain the prescribed levels of individual well-being with less of any good.

COMMUNITY INDIFFERENCE: THE BERGSON FRONTIER

The levels of individual well-being we prescribed in drawing up the Scitovsky frontier were chosen arbitrarily. If we choose another set of levels, we shall in general arrive at another frontier. There is no reason why it should not intersect the first. Proceeding in this way, we can obtain an infinity of Scitovsky frontiers, intersecting one another indefinitely often.

Now is the time to use the Bergson social welfare function, $W(u^1, \ldots, u^\nu)$. Let us assume that we are given a Pareto W—i.e. one for which a *cet. par.* increase in one man's welfare increases

† This remark is particularly relevant when individual indifference curves are 'wrongly' shaped—i.e. concave to the origin. Cf. the discussion of increasing returns in Chapter II; the last section of Chapter IV; and P. A. Samuelson, *Foundations of Economic Analysis* (Cambridge, Mass., 1947), p. 238.

social welfare—and let us consider one of its contours, which is a relation between the individual utility indicators obtained by putting

$$W(u^1, ..., u^\nu) = \text{constant}.$$

Now for any set of u's satisfying this relation we can draw up a Scitovsky community indifference curve. Indeed, for each of the infinity of sets of the u's satisfying the relation we can draw up such a curve. The matter is illustrated in Fig. 5, where but a few are sketched and labelled SS. The *inner limit* of the family of Scitovsky curves we shall call the *Bergson frontier*.† In Fig. 5*a*, where the SS curves are convex to the origin, it is the envelope of the family. In Fig. 5*b*, where the Scitovsky curves are not so well

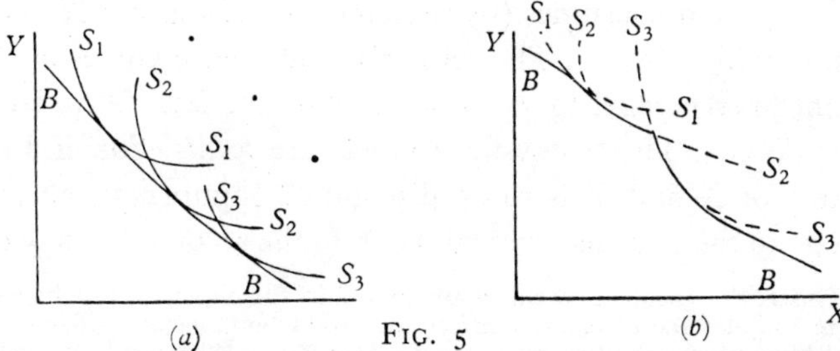

FIG. 5

behaved, it is no longer necessarily the true envelope—the 'true' envelope would typically be the *outer* limit of the family—but it is still the inner limit.

What does a Bergson frontier tell us? Given any amount of either X or Y, it tells us the minimum amount of the other good required to attain a given level of social welfare, as defined by W. It is thus a community indifference curve depicting *social tastes* (as defined by W) in the same way as a private one depicts personal tastes. Let us investigate some of its properties.

(1) At every point BB is touched by an SS curve (Fig. 5*a*) or

† Professor Bergson's fundamental paper ('A Reformulation of Certain Aspects of Welfare Economics', *Quarterly Journal of Economics*, vol. LII (1938), pp. 310–34) was published several years before community indifference curves came into vogue (largely as a result of Professor Scitovsky's cited paper). He naturally did not, therefore, apply his welfare function device to the problem of social indifference curves; but I do not think that the name 'Bergson frontier' is inappropriate.

coincides with one (Fig. 5*b*). At every point, therefore, our three conditions on marginal social rates of substitution (with respect to appropriate prescribed sets of individual indifference curves) must be satisfied.

(2) It is straightforward to show that, in the absence of external effects, individual indifference curves convex to the origin lead to convex Scitovsky frontiers.† There is not, however, any simple relation between the convexity of individual indifference curves and that of the Bergson frontiers—even in the absence of external effects. Bergson curves can be of any shape.

It is instructive to consider the very simple case where external effects are absent in a two-person, two-commodity world in which the first person consumes (by preference) nothing but X and the second nothing but Y. The former's indifference curves are then straight lines parallel to the Y-axis, while the latter's are parallel to the X-axis. The Scitovsky frontiers are *points*. For, if a combination of X and Y is to be distributed 'optimally', all the X must go to the first man and all the Y to the second. To any com-

† This is the analogue of the result (noted in the appendix to Chapter II) that, in the absence of external effects in production, society will encounter diminishing returns if all its members do. It is most easily seen by a modification of the well-known diagrammatic technique (to which we have referred) for constructing, in a two-commodity world, a social transformation function from two private ones. In Fig. 6, the first man's indifference curve (I') and the axes to which it is referred are drawn ordinarily, while the second man's (I'') and its axes are dotted. The position of O'' in relation to O' gives the minimum combination of X and Y required to keep the two men on their prescribed indifference curves (I' and I''). By sliding the dotted system in such a way that I' and I'' are always touching, O'' can be made to trace out a locus. It will be the relevant Scitovsky frontier. If I' and I'' are convex to their respective origins, the locus traced out by O'' will be convex to O'. The reader will have no difficulty in demonstrating this.

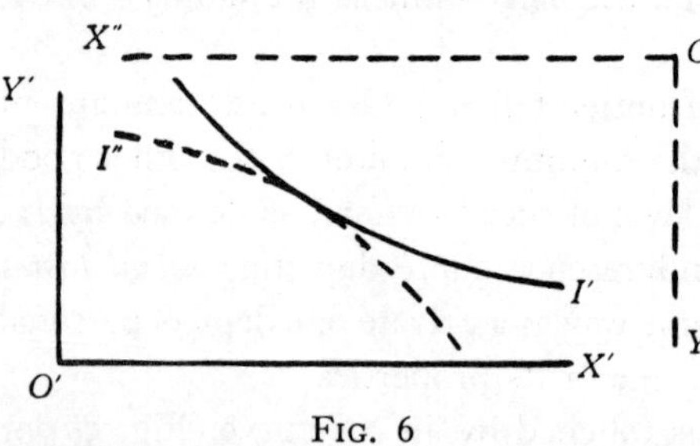

Fig. 6

It is instructive to experiment with indifference curves less well-behaved—and to try applying the technique to production. It will be observed that, because of the prevalence of boundary extrema (where one of the men consumes no X, or no Y), individual indifference curves concave to their respective origins can give Scitovsky frontiers of any shape.

bination of X and Y, 'optimally' distributed, there therefore corresponds a unique pair of levels of individual well-being. The Scitovsky frontier is thus a point. If we join all the points representing equal levels of social welfare, we shall obtain a non-intersecting family of Bergson curves. Their shape will clearly depend on the ethical judgements summarized in W, and on nothing else. They are sketched in Fig. 7*a*. The corresponding W contours are sketched in Fig. 7*b*.

(3) One important difference between Figs. 7*a* and 7*b* should be noted. For any Pareto W, the higher W contours in Fig. 7*b* represent levels of higher social welfare. This is, in general, not true of the BB curves in Fig. 7*a*. It is of course true in the very

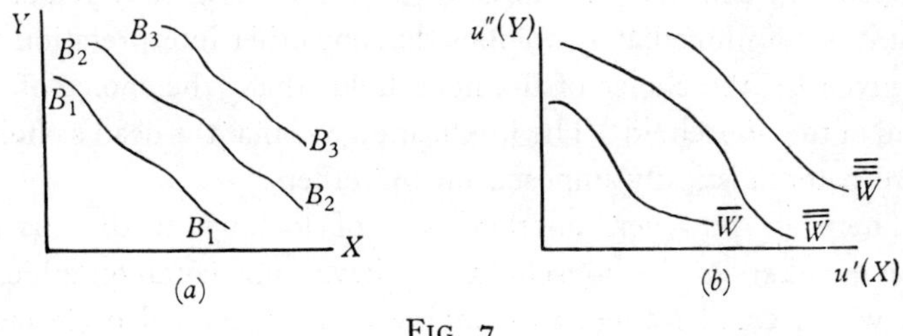

FIG. 7

simple model we have just been discussing, where external effects were ruled out by assumption. But, in the general case where external effects exist, it is conceivable that the envy and malice engendered by having more of *every* good—or simply the mysterious movement of fashion the new age of plenty brings forth—will leave society worse off, or no better off, than before. (Given that everyone else has atom bombs, my welfare may increase when I obtain one for myself. But everybody may feel better off if all bombs are destroyed overnight.) It will be convenient to have a name for this phenomenon. We shall refer to it by saying that the external effects in consumption are *excessive*.

Excessiveness may be unlikely, but it is conceivable. We cannot simply rule it out of court—although, by ignoring it in discussing the production and Scitovsky frontiers, we have implicitly done so up to now. We must recognize that higher BB curves (and higher

SS curves) may not represent higher levels of social welfare, and that they may slope upwards over certain ranges.

(4) Finally, a word about intersections. Welfare contours of the sort drawn in Fig. 6*b* can never intersect if we confine ourselves to Pareto *W*'s. When external effects are excessive, however, Bergson frontiers may intersect. Scitovsky frontiers, of course, can intersect whether or not external effects are excessive—whether or not they exist.

THE INDIVIDUAL AND THE HOUSEHOLD

Very frequently welfare economists use 'the members of the community' to mean the *households*—rather than the individual men, women and children—comprising it. We have already remarked that it is not immediately obvious that any other interpretation can be given to 'the choice of the household' than 'the choice of the head of the household'. The implication was that the head's choices were paternalistically imposed on the others.

There is, however, another way of looking at the matter. The members of the household may have some common ethic, or *W*, which enables them to combine their individual preference-scales into a household scale. It is, indeed, more probable that a sufficient consilience of ethical valuations will exist within a small household than throughout a large nation—a clearly defined *W* is more likely to exist for one household than for a number of households. If this be granted, the 'private indifference curves' of the household are nothing else than Bergson frontiers. They may not behave very well—especially since external effects are likely to be extremely important within a household—but if we assume the household to come into equilibrium at fixed prices on a competitive market, we can place various familiar restrictions on their shape in the neighbourhood of potential equilibrium points.

There is nothing formally wrong with this way of looking at the matter, but the paternalist approach does seem to be the more realistic. Households are rare, I should say, in which the preference-scales of the children are fully incorporated into a welfare function of the individualist type.

APPENDIX TO CHAPTER III

The construction of a *Scitovsky frontier* from a prescribed set of individual indifference curves is, from a formal point of view, precisely the same problem as the construction of a social transformation function from a set of private ones. We need, therefore, do little more than refer to the appendix to Chapter II.

Let us maintain the convention that rendering productive services is negative consumption of goods, and write x_i^α for the quantity of the ith good consumed by the αth man. We define X_i by

$$X_i = \sum_\alpha x_i^\alpha \qquad (i = 1, \ldots, n) \qquad (1)$$

so that it is the community's net consumption of the ith good.†

Each of the ν members of the community has a utility function, which we shall write $u^\theta(x)$, $(\theta = 1, \ldots, \nu)$. The argument, x, is a row vector of x_i^α, $(i = 1, \ldots, n; \alpha = 1, \ldots, \nu)$. When external effects are non-existent, we have u^θ independent of x_i^α for $\alpha \neq \theta$. Let us denote the prescribed set of individual indifference curves by $\{c_1, \ldots, c_\nu\}$, so that their equations are

$$u^\alpha(x) - c_\alpha = 0. \qquad (\alpha = 1, \ldots, \nu) \qquad (2)$$

We seek a relation between the X_i of the form

$$S(X_1, \ldots, X_n) = 0 \qquad (3)$$

which will tell us the *minimum* value any one can take, given the values of the remaining ones, if each man is to remain on his prescribed indifference curve—i.e. if the equations (2) are to be satisfied.

We can now proceed exactly as in the appendix to Chapter II. We seek minimum, rather than maximum, values—but that is of no consequence. The first-order conditions are the same as before—they lead to the familiar rules about marginal social rates of substitution—and so are the integrability conditions. There is nothing to add.

When we want to construct the *Bergson frontier*, we seek a relation between the X_i of the form

$$B(X_1, \ldots, X_n) = 0 \qquad (4)$$

which will tell us the minimum value any one can take, given the values of the remaining ones, if the equation

$$W(u^1, \ldots, u^\nu) = \overline{W} \qquad (5)$$

† There is no loss of generality, and great convenience, in abstracting from collective goods in the present context. For them we have

$$X_i = x_i^1 = \cdots = x_i^\nu$$

The reader will verify that their inclusion would in no way affect the substance of what follows.

is to be satisfied. The single equation (5) then takes the place of the ν equations (2) in the above procedure. For the rest, we proceed exactly as before. The demonstration that B is, under certain conditions, the envelope of a family of S's, defined by $W=\overline{W}$, is both straightforward and unnecessary.

One result is worth noting explicitly. It is the analogue of equation (9) of the appendix to Chapter II. We have

$$\frac{\partial B/\partial X_i}{\partial B/\partial X_j}=\left(\frac{\partial W/\partial x_i^\alpha}{\partial W/\partial x_j^\beta}\right)_{\overline{W}}. \qquad \begin{matrix}(i, j=1, \ldots, n)\\ (\alpha, \beta=1, \ldots, \nu)\end{matrix} \tag{6}$$

Excessive external effects exist whenever one (or both) of the first partial derivatives of W is negative. When both are negative, the Bergson frontier slopes downwards as usual, but higher frontiers represent lower levels of social welfare. When they differ in sign, the frontier slopes upwards. Observe that the marginal social rates of indifference defined by this equation depend explicitly on the welfare function used. Interpersonal comparisons are therefore involved in determining them. If, however, we assume that external effects do not exist in consumption, the right-hand side of equation (6) simplifies considerably. We then have

$$\frac{\partial B/\partial X_i}{\partial B/\partial X_j}=\frac{\partial u^1/\partial x_i^1}{\partial u^1/\partial x_j^1}=\cdots\cdots=\frac{\partial u^\nu/\partial x_i^\nu}{\partial u^\nu/\partial x_j^\nu}. \tag{7}$$

Marginal social and private rates of indifference coincide. No interpersonal comparisons are now involved.

Note too that our procedure for constructing a Bergson frontier comes to exactly the same thing as fixing the amounts of the X_i of (1), and maximizing W subject to these constraints. Thus when it is said that society is on the Bergson frontier it is equivalent to saying that a fixed collection of goods is 'optimally distributed' among its members.

CHAPTER IV

POTENTIAL WELFARE

The results of the last two chapters can rapidly be combined. They lead to a statement of the necessary conditions for the General Optimum of Production and Exchange—due essentially to Pareto, but implicit in much of Pigou's 'particular equilibrium' analysis.† Indeed, it might be said that Pigou's treatment is in a sense the more 'general', since he is the more aware of external effects—especially in production.

Before we start it is as well to note that we require a well-defined *horizon*. Our social transformation function is defined with reference to it, and so are the individual utility functions of the members of the community. Moreover, the observing economist is assumed to know the composition of the community—the tastes of the men who will die and of the men who will be born—during the whole course of future time this side of the horizon. Only on this assumption can we proceed. The problem of actually determining the horizon we leave for Chapter VI. We shall also postpone till then discussion of the amounts of *terminal* capital equipment to be left over when the horizon is attained. For the present we shall assume them given.

THE GENERAL OPTIMUM

In Fig. 8 the *BB* curves are social indifference curves (of the 'Bergson frontier' type) corresponding to any Paretian welfare function. *TT* is the social production frontier, assumed to be independent of the distribution of wealth. In the first diagram both *X* and *Y* are outputs; in the second, *X* is an input—but the argument is quite general. What are the conditions for maximum welfare?

Let us start by abstracting from excessive external effects in

† For a vivid account of the growth of the theory of the General Optimum in the writings of the 'marginal utility economists', see Hla Myint, *Theories of Welfare Economics* (London, 1948), Chap. VII.

consumption. The Bergson curves must then slope downwards in Fig. 8*a* and upwards in Fig. 8*b*. They cannot intersect; and higher ones must represent higher levels of social welfare. The highest level of social welfare will be attained either in a 'boundary maximum' (Fig. 8*a*) or, if the curves are suitably smooth, in a point of tangency (Fig. 8*b*). In both diagrams the maximum is labelled *M*.

Tangency of the two frontiers is equivalent to the *equality of marginal social rates of transformation and indifference*. Moreover, society is actually on both its frontiers at *M*. *The two sets of necessary marginal conditions we set out in Chapters II and III must therefore also be satisfied.*

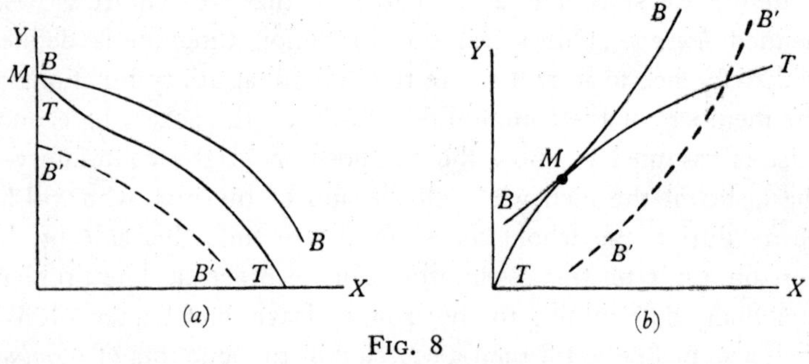

FIG. 8

Consider now a boundary maximum. Society is still on both its frontiers, so the two sets of marginal conditions must still be satisfied. However, one good is neither produced nor consumed—although it could be produced and although it enters into individual preference-scales. In formal language this can be phrased in terms of the marginal social rate of indifference being greater than the rate of transformation. But it is simpler to say that the amount of *Y* which would have to be sacrificed to obtain an incipient amount of *X* is greater than is consistent with maintaining each member of the community at the prescribed level of well-being. Note that this has no necessary connection with increasing returns (i.e. with the convexity of *TT* to the origin), but is solely dependent on the *relative* curvature of *TT* and *BB*. It is thus essentially bound up with the ethical judgements summarized in the welfare function defining BB (and prescribing the levels of individual well-being).

It is most important to observe, however, that the necessary conditions for the General Optimum—whether they give boundary maxima or not—are put in terms which make no reference whatsoever to a particular welfare function. They involve rates of transformation and indifference, and nothing else. They are valid for any Pareto W—for any set of ethical judgements which lets a *cet. par.* increase in one man's welfare increase social welfare. They are valid, that is to say,† even if interpersonal comparisons of well-being are declared 'impossible'. This is the chief significance of the General Optimum. We cannot have an optimum in terms of a Pareto W unless its marginal equivalences are fulfilled. That is to say: if they are *not* fulfilled—if the General Optimum is *not* attained—*we can make everybody better off*.

Pareto's achievement in formulating the necessary conditions for the attainment of the General Optimum in terms independent of interpersonal comparisons of well-being was a considerable one. But he confined himself to the case where external effects did not exist. In the more general formulation we have given, the appearance of independence of interpersonal comparisons is largely specious. When external effects are absent from consumption, social and private rates of indifference coincide and are quite unambiguously determined by the individual utility functions. But when external effects are not absent from consumption, we do not know what the social rates of indifference are until we have selected a prescribed set of individual indifference curves—or until we are given a social welfare function. Interpersonal comparisons enter at this stage of the procedure—in defining social rates of indifference.

The General Optimum nevertheless remains an important concept. The marginal conditions characterizing it may involve interpersonal comparisons whenever external effects make themselves felt in consumption, but its significance is otherwise unimpaired: when it is not attained, everybody can be made better off. Pareto's

† Cf. Chapter I.

celebrated *maximum d'utilité collective*—which obtains only when it is impossible to make any one man better off without making at least one other worse off—naturally entails it. Let us proceed to complete the picture by introducing various complications.

(1) The familiar marginal equalities (and inequalities) are necessary for the attainment of the General Optimum as far as final consumer's goods are concerned. They apply not only to goods a man purchases for himself, but also to collective goods and to advertising—they apply to all the variables entering the individual utility functions out of which the Bergson frontiers are constructed.

But what happens to *producers' goods*? They do not enter directly into preference-scales, and cannot therefore be discussed in terms of the diagrams of Fig. 8. Their optimal production is determined, however, as soon as we know the social transformation function and the inputs and outputs of goods which do enter directly into consumers' preference-scales.† We have another familiar marginal equality: inputs must be transferred to the production (and maintenance) of producers' goods, and outputs sacrificed on their behalf, until the loss resulting from a further transference or sacrifice just balances the gain—both loss and gain being measured in terms of any consumers' good. The optimal rate of investment (or capital accumulation) this side of the horizon is thus implicitly determined.

(2) What happens to the General Optimum when we admit the possibility of excessive external effects in consumption? Not only can the Bergson frontiers intersect, and slope the 'wrong' way, but the highest level of social welfare is typically attained on a curve like $B'B'$ in Fig. 8. The familiar marginal equalities are no longer necessary. The optimum need not lie on the production frontier. The fundamental value judgement of Chapter II, that it is desirable to have a *cet. par.* increase in the output of any good, is no longer compatible with a Pareto W. There may be an infinite number of attainable optima. Any point on $B'B'$ represents the same maximum level of social welfare; an infinity of these are within TT, and are

† Cf. appendix to this chapter, equation (4).

therefore attainable. Uniqueness is not, however, necessarily ruled out. There is no reason why the Bergson frontiers should not be closed curves centreing on some unique point within TT, like the contours of a hill whose summit represents the maximum.

(3) Finally, it should be noted that the familiar marginal equalities of the General Optimum also break down if we admit that the social transformation function may depend upon the distribution of wealth. Certain rather more complicated marginal conditions hold, but these are best left for the appendix.

THE WELFARE FRONTIER

We are now ready for the last of the various 'frontiers' we shall find it useful to employ. Consider for geometrical simplicity a community of but two people, Alpha and Beta. Their utility indicators, u^α and u^β, we shall write α and β for short. No special significance attaches to the particular indexes selected; but, once adopted, they must be adhered to without change.

Let us fix β at some arbitrary level, say β_0, and make Alpha as well off as is possible under the circumstances. Just how great a value α will be able to attain will depend upon (i) the value β_0; (ii) the supply of goods and services available to the community; and (iii) the possibility of transforming goods and services of one kind into goods of another kind. This transformation can be performed in factories at home, or by trade with communities abroad—but we abstract from foreign trade for the present. The utility and social transformation functions therefore effectively summarize items (ii) and (iii). They determine a unique maximum value of α, say α_0, corresponding to β_0.

If we fix β at some other level, we shall obtain another level of α. Proceeding in this way, we can map out a locus in the (α, β)-plane. We shall call it the community's *welfare frontier*. It has been independently introduced to welfare theory by M. Allais † and Professor Samuelson,‡ who calls it the 'utility-possibility

† M. Allais, *A la Recherche d'une Discipline Économique*, tome I (printed for private circulation, Paris, 1943), pp. 604 ff.

‡ Paul A. Samuelson, *Foundations of Economic Analysis* (Cambridge, Mass., 1947), pp. 243 ff.

function'†—just as a production frontier is sometimes called a 'production-possibility function'. Let us set out its properties:

(1) In the general multi-person community of any size, the welfare frontier tells us the maximum level of well-being any one man can enjoy, given the levels enjoyed by the remaining members of the community. It represents society's *welfare potential*, just as the social production frontier represents its productive potential. Its significance hinges on the fact that, while no point outside it is attainable by society with the existing 'state of the arts', no point lying inside it can ever represent a maximum of social welfare in terms of any Pareto W. For to any interior point (like

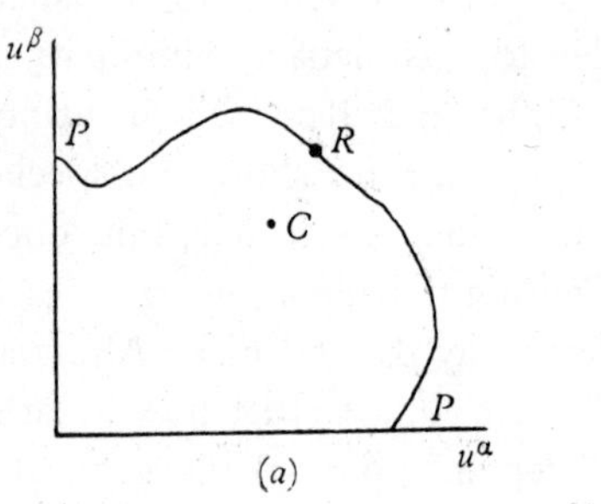

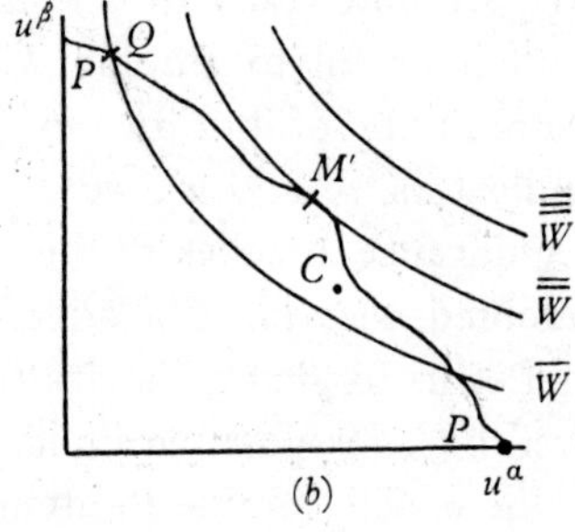

FIG. 9

C in Fig. 9*a*) there necessarily corresponds a better point (like R) on the frontier (labelled PP). It is 'better' in terms of any Pareto W, since both Alpha and Beta are better off.

(2) If, as in Fig. 9*b*, we sketch in the contours of some Paretian functions, $W(u^\alpha, u^\beta)$, we can find the point (or points) in which the highest level of social welfare is attained. If we use the W with reference to which the BB curves of Fig. 8 were drawn up, the point M' on the welfare frontier in Fig. 9*b* indicates the levels of individual well-being secured by distributing in an optimal way the optimal collection of goods determined by the production and Bergson frontiers in Fig. 8. In terms of the classical Cambridge W (which regards social welfare as the sum of the cardinal utilities

† In my paper 'On Optimum Tariff Structures', *Review of Economic Studies*, vol. XVII (1) (1949–50), I used the term 'possibility locus'. I now think, however, that 'welfare frontier' is more appropriate.

of the members of the community), M' is the point at which the 'marginal utility of income' is the same for both Alpha and Beta.

(3) The shape, curvature and position of the welfare frontier depend upon the particular indexes selected to represent individual levels of well-being—for convenience it has been drawn in the north-east quadrant in Fig. 9. But the *direction of slope* is invariant. It will 'normally' slope downwards: Alpha can be made better off only at Beta's expense. 'Occasionally', however, it may slope upwards. Three cases deserve especial notice:

(i) The first is where the social transformation function depends markedly upon the distribution of wealth. If workers are underfed, a redistribution of wealth in their favour may so increase efficiency that everybody benefits.† In such cases the frontier will slope upwards. One might suppose, on crude empirical grounds, that this is likely only when there is *extreme* inequality in the distribution of wealth.

(ii) External effects in consumption can bring about the same result. There is no need for them to be excessive. Consider first a two-person community. External economies in consumption may be so marked and asymmetrical that a transfer of goods from Alpha to Beta increases the welfare of each. In a genuine two-person community one would expect such situations to be unstable, Alpha simply making Beta a gift. In a larger community, however, stability might plausibly be assumed.

(iii) In a larger community, moreover, external *dis*economies can give the frontier an upward slope. Demonstration of this can be left for the appendix and a footnote.‡

† Cf. appendix to this chapter, equation (12).

‡ Consider a community comprising Alpha, Beta and Gamma. Assume that Alpha's welfare is uninfluenced by the goods possessed by either Beta or Gamma, and that they in turn are uninfluenced by Alpha's possessions. But assume, too, that marked external diseconomies exist between Beta and Gamma. Then, if we are interested in the slope of the frontier in the (α, β)-plane, we must examine the rate at which β changes when α is diminished slightly by a transfer of goods from Alpha to Beta, when γ (Gamma's utility indicator) is kept constant. But the increase in Beta's possessions makes Gamma worse off, so to keep γ constant it is necessary to transfer some to Gamma. This, however, makes Beta worse off on two scores: firstly, because the goods are taken from him, and, secondly, because Gamma's increase. It is easy to construct examples along these lines in which the original small decrease in α causes β to decrease too, γ being kept

When the frontier slopes upwards over a certain range there is not perfect symmetry in its definition. This is clear from Fig. 9*a*. We get one result when we choose to hold α constant, and maximize β; another when we reverse the procedure. The first will give β as a single-valued function of α; the second α as a single-valued function of β. The complete frontier is obtained by combining the two (i.e. by holding each constant in turn) to obtain what will in general be a multi-valued function of α, β, or both.

The importance of the direction of slope of the frontier is considerable, for (if we confine ourselves to Pareto *W*'s) we can rule out those parts which slope upwards as positions of maximum welfare. When it slopes upwards we can make everybody better off. In a sense, therefore, we can speak of the (possibly discontinuous) downward-sloping section as the 'true' welfare frontier; and we can also speak of a sense in which the distribution of real income is 'not optimal' on upward-sloping sections of the frontier.

(4) Any point on a downward-sloping portion of the frontier represents a Paretian *maximum d'utilité collective*—or, put in our own terminology, is a potential optimum in terms of a Pareto *W*. Barring excessive external effects in consumption, therefore, *all the familiar marginal equivalences of the General Optimum must be satisfied* at any point on a downward-sloping section.

Moreover, although the reasoning is less straightforward, they must hold on upward-sloping sections too. This is most easily seen by glancing at the appendix. The length of a verbal demonstration seems to be out of proportion to the importance of the result. It happens that the same marginal conditions are entailed if (i) we fix the levels of well-being of all men but one, and make the remaining man as well off as possible, or (ii) we look for positions in which it is impossible to make any one man better off

constant—i.e. where the frontier slopes upwards in the (α, β)-plane. The marked external diseconomies we assumed to exist between Beta and Gamma can secure this result in spite of the fact that after the decrease in α they both possess (in physical terms) more wealth than before. Cf. appendix to this chapter, equations (13), (14) and the following discussion.

without making at least one other worse off. The first procedure leads us to the 'complete' welfare frontier; the second to the 'true' one, which (though possibly discontinuous) slopes downwards everywhere.

(5) To move on to the welfare frontier, therefore, it is necessary to secure the satisfaction of the marginal equivalences of the General Optimum. How are movements *along* the frontier secured? Clearly, they are secured by redistributions of wealth which do not destroy the marginal equivalences. Such redistributions we shall call *lump-sum*.

(6) What happens to the collection of goods produced by society's transformation process as we move along the welfare frontier? Generally speaking, it will change. We saw in (2) that to a point on the frontier like M' in Fig. 9*b* there corresponds an optimal collection of goods, like that represented by M in Fig. 8. If we consider a different point, there will usually correspond a different collection of goods.

Let us start from a point like M', and fix the collection of goods. Let us redistribute these goods among the members of the community by lump-sum measures. What happens? A new welfare frontier (corresponding to the fixed collection of goods) is traced out. It cannot lie outside the 'proper' one, PP, as that represents the best we can do when we take into account the possibilities of transforming goods and services of one kind into goods of another (and preferred) kind. It must, therefore, lie wholly inside PP, touching it in M' (and perhaps elsewhere). If we shift our starting-point on PP from M' to some other point, and again fix the collection of goods, we can trace out another welfare frontier, also lying wholly within PP, by lump-sum redistributions. These *exchange-economy* welfare frontiers—as we shall call those traced out by lump-sum redistributions of various fixed collections of goods—are infinitely many. Their *outer limit* (or envelope) is the 'proper' frontier, or *production-economy* welfare frontier, drawn with reference to the production possibilities open to society, and not just for a given collection of goods. This distinction is worth noting, as we return to it in later chapters.

POTENTIAL BENEFIT†

A movement from a point like C inside the welfare frontier to one like Q on it does not necessarily represent an increase in welfare (Fig. 9*b*). There is no reason why Q should not lie on a lower welfare contour than C. But we can (and shall) say that Q is *potentially* better than C, for there necessarily exists a point on the frontier (like R in Fig. 9*a*) in which both Alpha and Beta are better off and to which a mere redistribution of wealth can lead us.

Similarly, if we confine ourselves to positions actually on the welfare-frontier—the more general situation is discussed in the next chapter—we can define the *potential desirability* of a change such as might result from technological 'progress' or some other movement of the social production function. There are two distinct possibilities: (i) on the one hand, the new welfare frontier may lie wholly inside, or wholly outside, the old one. Such a movement we shall refer to as a *shift*. It is illustrated by $P_1'P_1''$ in Fig. 10, which lies wholly outside $P_0'\,P_0''$. Any position on the new frontier is clearly at least potentially superior to any position on the old one. Thus the technological 'progress' can be said to be at least potentially beneficial; (ii) on the other hand, the new frontier may intersect the old one. This is represented by $P_2'\,P_2''$ in Fig. 10, where the intersection is in X. We shall refer to it as a *twist*. All that can be said is that the situations on $P_2'X$ are at least potentially superior to those on $P_0'X$; and that those on $P_0''X$ are at least potentially superior to those on $P_2''X$. We cannot say that the technological 'progress' is even potentially beneficial until we are given some criterion on the basis of which we can judge between situations on $P_2'X$ and those on $P_0''X$—some criterion for making interpersonal comparisons of

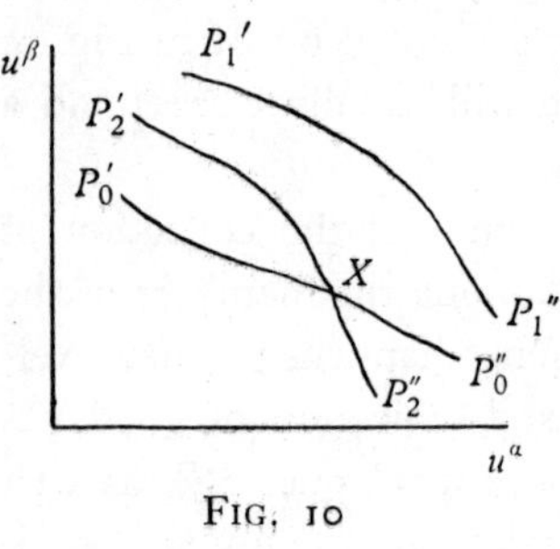

FIG. 10

† Cf. P. A. Samuelson, *Foundations of Economic Analysis* (Cambridge, Mass., 1947), pp. 250–2, to which I am heavily indebted.

well-being. In this simple case a very simple criterion—a very incompletely defined *W*—is sufficient: we only need to compare two broad and distinct distributions of welfare (P'_2X and P''_0X). In the general case, however, we should probably require a well-defined *W* to be able to discriminate: there is no reason why the frontiers should not intersect infinitely often. But, when we have a well-defined *W*, we can examine quite directly the desirability of any change—we need not rest content with statements about *potentialities*. It is important to note this point.

The essential indeterminacy which, in the absence of a well-defined *W*, arises whenever the frontier twists, seems at first sight to make the whole concept a rather clumsy one. To a certain extent this is true. It is not easy to find instances of unambiguous shifts in a welfare frontier. A uniform shift in the social production frontier will naturally translate itself into a similar movement of the welfare one (unless we have excessive external effects in consumption), but that is not very helpful. We shall see in Chapter IX that the imposition of taxes of a certain size on both imports and exports will always shift the welfare frontier outwards, and can never twist it sufficiently for it to intersect with its former position. Apart from these examples, however, we are very much in the dark.

Moreover, there are several points to be remembered when using the concept of 'potential benefit'. Firstly, it is only relevant to Pareto *W*'s. Secondly, the whole discussion is 'comparative statical'. The change whose potential desirability we examine must not take place through time. (Intertemporal changes involve special problems which are reserved for Chapter XI.) We compare two conjectural or hypothetical situations at a given moment of time. Thirdly, we can really only apply the concept to changes which operate through production (or foreign trade)—it could yield no results if we were to discuss, for example, problems relating to the 'optimum population', for when the population changes, our standards of reference (individual tastes) change too. Finally, we must assume throughout that the time horizon and the terminal capital equipment are somehow given.

CORRECTIVE TAXES AND COMPETITION

We have already recorded two familiar facts about perfect competition, corrected by suitable taxes. It can be made so to harness the profit-seeking efforts of private producers that the social production frontier is attained; and the mechanism which operates when consumers trade at fixed prices (which just clear the market) can so allocate a given collection of goods that the highest Bergson frontier is attained. It remains to record the equally familiar fact that it can, under certain circumstances, also lead society to its welfare frontier. That is to say: not only can it secure the optimal organization of production in the engineering sense, and the optimal distribution of a fixed collection of goods, but it can secure that the 'fixed' collection of goods produced is itself an optimal collection.

The demonstration is straightforward. The market price-ratios facing producers, and to which they are cajoled (by corrective taxes) into equating marginal social rates of transformation, are the same as those which face private consumers, and to which they are cajoled into equating marginal social rates of indifference. Marginal social rates of transformation and indifference are thus equal. Moreover, a private producer will transfer resources from current production to investment until the net gain from a further transfer is zero. All the marginal equivalences necessary (in the absence of excessiveness) for the attainment of the General Optimum, and thus the welfare frontier, are achieved.† At least, they are achieved as far as purchasable goods are concerned: collective ones are usually assumed to be handled by the ballot, rather than by the ordinary mechanism of the market.

That is how the argument usually runs. There are, however, four cases where it breaks down, and where further corrective devices are required to save the situation. To emphasize that none of them have anything to do with external effects or interpersonal

† For simplicity, boundary optima (where certain *inequalities* have to be satisfied) are ignored. The reader will have no trouble in completing the outlines of the argument for himself. Some points of difficulty, where the inequalities will not be satisfied by perfect competition (unless corrected by further taxes), are discussed in detail below.

comparisons (though these may make their occurrence more likely), let us consider a one-man community—or a community in which men are identical in all respects. The *II*-curves of Fig. 11 are thus ordinary individual indifference curves. *TT* is the production frontier; and in both diagrams maximum welfare is attained in *M*.

(*a*) In Fig. 11*a* no *X* is produced or consumed in the position of maximum welfare. To persuade producers to concentrate on *Y*, and produce no *X*, it is necessary to make *X* very cheap relatively to *Y*. The slope of the dotted *MA* gives the limiting price ratio; but, if it were established, consumers would want to purchase

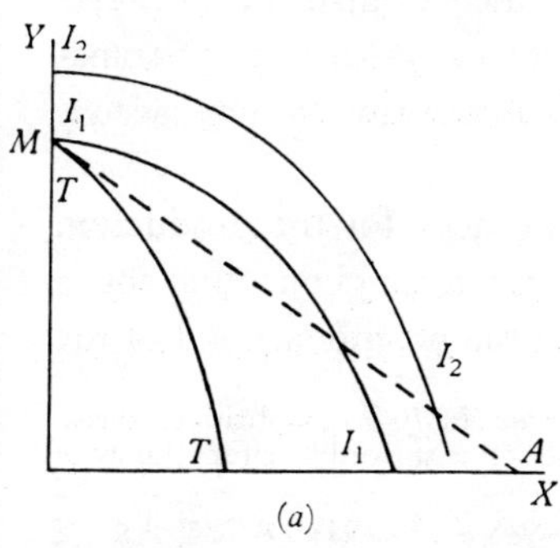

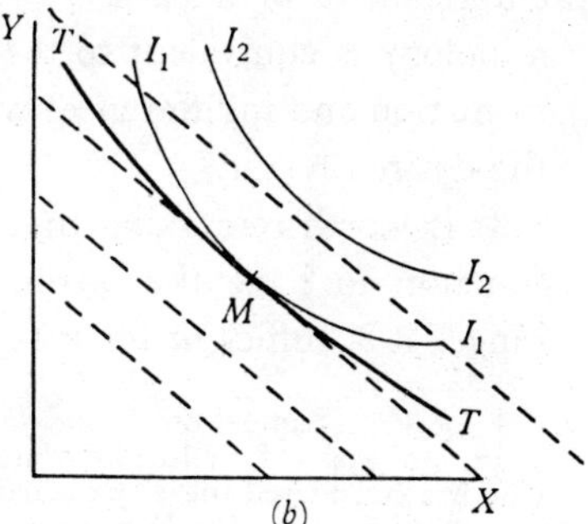

FIG. 11

much *X*, and no *Y*. To persuade consumers to demand no *X*, it is necessary to make it very dear relatively to *Y*. Producers require a low ratio, consumers a high one. A meeting-point may not exist. If it does not, another corrective tax is needed. At first sight this may appear paradoxical, but that is simply because we are unaccustomed to thinking of cases where the curvature of the individual indifference curves is 'wrong'—i.e. unfavourable to perfect competition.†

(*b*) In Fig. 11*b* we have the case where the curvature of the

† The reader accustomed to thinking in monetary terms may wonder why, if producers are prepared to produce for less than consumers are prepared to pay, welfare would not be increased by expanding (or permitting) production. He need simply remind himself, however, that this type of reasoning is only valid if we can assume a 'constant marginal utility of money'. Here that assumption would clearly be inadmissible.

production function is 'wrong'.† It depicts increasing returns—or decreasing marginal (opportunity) costs. The point of maximum welfare, M, would be a position of *minimum*, not maximum, profit to a firm facing fixed market prices. (The dotted parallel lines are contours showing combinations of X and Y which yield a firm the same net return. Their slope is the price ratio.) To persuade a profit-seeking entrepreneur to produce at M, it would be necessary to devise corrective measures (such as *ad valorem* taxes at a variable rate) which would convert M into a point of maximum profit by distorting the dotted contours in a suitable way. It is rather difficult to imagine this being done in practice; but the enforcement of Professor Lerner's 'rule' (which in our terminology is equivalent to the equality of marginal rates of transformation and indifference) would, it is interesting to note, secure the desired result.‡

It is worth remarking that there is no need for the production function to have the 'wrong' curvature throughout the entire range; it is sufficient for it to have it in the neighbourhood of the

† Cf. P. A. Samuelson, *Foundations of Economic Analysis* (Cambridge, Mass., 1947), pp. 234–5, for a lucid discussion. Samuelson is the only writer I know of who has considered these 'paradoxical' cases.

‡ A. P. Lerner, *The Economics of Control* (New York, 1944), *passim*. Lerner does not, however, consider this case where the operation of the rule would entail minimum, rather than maximum, profits—for he explicitly assumes constant returns *to scale*. It is well known (cf. P. A. Samuelson, 'International Factor-Price Equalization Once Again', *Economic Journal*, vol. LIX (1949), pp. 184–5) that, in the absence of external effects in production, constant returns to scale entail that the transformation curve between any two outputs is concave to the origin. (Lerner phrases this in terms of 'wise production avoiding increasing returns'—i.e. increasing *relative* returns as the proportion in which the factors are employed is varied—since, where it operates, one of the factors must have a *negative* marginal product (*op. cit.* p. 161).) It is easy to show that diminishing returns to scale simply reinforce this concavity to the origin. The transformation curve cannot, therefore, have the 'wrong' curvature unless we admit external effects or increasing returns to scale somewhere in the economy.

I relegate this whole matter to a footnote because I see no reason why we should make any particular assumption about *returns to scale*. Why should output double simply because we double all measurable inputs? Some of the constant-returns-to-scale fans seem to argue as though output would double if only we doubled *all* the 'inputs'—i.e. including non-measurable ones like 'organization', 'uncertainty-bearing' or entrepreneurship. But how can we 'double' the amounts of non-measurable inputs? There is no reason why constant (or diminishing) returns to scale should prevail. We cannot, on *a priori* grounds alone, rule out the possibility of the transformation function having a curvature unfavourable to competition. (Cf. Samuelson, *op. cit.* pp. 84–5.)

optimum point. Readers accustomed to thinking of the equilibrium of the firm under competitive conditions in terms of the intersection of the price-line with the marginal (money) cost curve may find this suggestive. For competitive equilibrium to obtain, the marginal cost curve must slope upwards where it cuts the price-line. But it need not slope upwards everywhere; and there is no reason why the 'ideal' output (from a welfare point of view) should conveniently occur on an upward-sloping section of the curve.

(*c*) The third and fourth cases in which perfect competition fails to secure the marginal equivalence of the General Optimum require little elaboration. In Fig. 12*a* we have a 'correctly' shaped

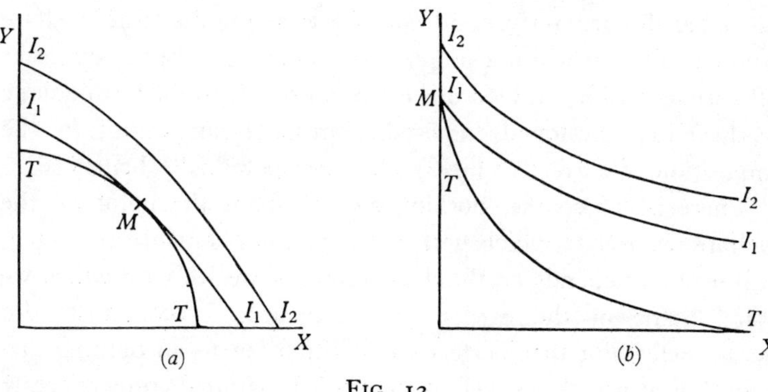

FIG. 12

production function giving a non-boundary maximum, M, with a 'wrongly' shaped indifference curve. A consumer faced with fixed market prices would concentrate on either X or Y. No fixed price ratio could succeed in making him purchase some of each. But rationing, or a variable corrective tax (i.e. a variable *ad valorem* rate of tax, so that the consumer's budget line becomes curvilinear), could rectify the situation. Again, this seems curious simply because economists have for some reason concentrated attention on preference fields with just that shape which is favourable to competition.

(*d*) Fig. 12*b* requires little explanation. The indifference curves are 'correctly' shaped, but the production function shows increasing returns. As in case (*a*), depicted in Fig. 11*a*, a price which makes it profitable for producers to switch from X to Y *may* be so low that consumers' demands for X are greater than zero. A corrective tax is required. Note that while this is a possible consequence of increasing returns, it is not a necessary one. It depends on the relative steepness of the curves.

If the corrective taxes levied in the four cases we have just discussed abstract the whole, or more than the whole, of an entrepreneur's profit (or if his maximum profit is for some reason negative), a lump-sum payment will have to be made to him to keep him in business. But, assuming that this is done, and that the other corrective devices are zealously applied, perfect competition can be made to secure the satisfaction of the sufficient, as well as the necessary, conditions for attaining the 'true' welfare frontier. Then it will not be possible to make any one man better off without making at least one other worse off. In the terminology we have just developed, the establishment of competition (or the imposition of corrective taxes) is at least potentially beneficial.

There is, of course, nothing special about the point on the welfare frontier to which perfect competition, suitably corrected, will lead. It depends on the distribution of wealth with which we start. Some of the earlier 'marginal utility' economists did occasionally hint that perfect competition led to an optimal distribution of wealth, as well as to optimal marginal equivalences.† But the point on the welfare frontier which is 'the best' clearly depends on the particular W selected. It is a matter of ethics, not of competition. The important fact is simply that the ethical optimum can be realized in a suitable competitive environment by moving along the welfare frontier to wherever desired—by imposing lump-sum taxes which leave the marginal equivalences of the General Optimum unimpaired.

† See the remarks of Walker and J. B. Clark quoted in F. Y. Edgeworth, *Papers Relating to Political Economy*, vol. I (1925), pp. 51 ff.

APPENDIX TO CHAPTER IV

As before, we shall write the ν individual utility indicators

$$u^\theta = u^\theta(x). \qquad (\theta = 1, \ldots, \nu) \qquad (1)$$

The social transformation function, which we shall at first assume to depend upon the distribution of wealth, is conveniently written

$$T(x) = 0. \qquad (2)$$

In both (1) and (2) the argument, x, is a row vector of x_i^α, ($\alpha = 1, \ldots, \nu$; $i = 1, \ldots, n$), indicating the consumption of the ith good by the αth man.

We seek to maximize $W(u^1, \ldots, u^\nu)$, subject to the technological restraint (2). The first-order conditions are

$$\sum_\theta \frac{\partial W}{\partial u^\theta}\frac{\partial u^\theta}{\partial x_i^\alpha} + \mu \frac{\partial T}{\partial x_i^\alpha} = 0, \qquad \begin{matrix}(\alpha = 1, \ldots, \nu)\\(i = 1, \ldots, n)\end{matrix} \qquad (3)$$

where μ is a Lagrange multiplier. There are in (3) and (2) $n\nu + 1$ equations to determine the $n\nu$ x_i^α and μ.

Note that we get analogous first-order conditions if we maximize, subject to (2), each in turn of the u^θ of (1), keeping on each occasion the remaining ones constant. We have

$$\sum_\theta \lambda^\theta \frac{\partial u^\theta}{\partial x_i^\alpha} + \mu' \frac{\partial T}{\partial x_i^\alpha} = 0, \qquad \begin{matrix}(\alpha = 1, \ldots, \nu)\\(i = 1, \ldots, n)\end{matrix} \qquad (3')$$

where μ' and $(\nu - 1)$ of the λ^θ are Lagrange multipliers. The remaining λ is of course identically equal to unity. We have now $n\nu + 1$ equations in (3′) and (2), and an additional $(\nu - 1)$ indicating the levels at which the u^θ of (1) are held constant. Together, these are sufficient to determine the x_i^α, μ' and the λ^θ.

Whether we use (3) or (3′) depends largely on the problem in hand. The former is the more convenient for illustrating the text's discussion of the General Optimum. The latter seems to be the natural one to use when defining the welfare frontier, as it leads to the 'complete' frontier. The former selects the downward-sloping sections, and leads to the 'true' frontier only.

THE GENERAL OPTIMUM

Producers' goods do not enter the utility functions of the members of the community. If we typify them by X_p, equation (3) immediately reduces to

$$\partial T / \partial X_p = 0. \qquad (4)$$

This is the typical marginal condition determining their optimum outputs. For all variables which do enter the utility functions, however, we can write equation (3) in the form

$$\frac{\partial T/\partial x_i^\alpha}{\partial T/\partial x_j^\beta} = \frac{\partial W/\partial x_i^\alpha}{\partial W/\partial x_j^\beta} \qquad \begin{matrix} (\alpha, \beta = 1, \ldots, \nu) \\ (i, j = 1, \ldots, n) \end{matrix} \tag{5}$$

which we can interpret as the familiar equality of marginal social rates of transformation and indifference.

Now, maintaining the notation

$$X_i = \sum_\alpha x_i^\alpha$$

for all goods purchased by members of the community, and

$$X_i = x_i^1 = \cdot \cdot \cdot \cdot \cdot = x_i^\nu$$

for collective goods and advertising, let us assume that

$$\frac{\partial T}{\partial X_i} = \frac{\partial T}{\partial x_i^1} = \cdot \cdot \cdot \cdot \cdot = \frac{\partial T}{\partial x_i^\nu}. \qquad (i = 1, \ldots, n) \tag{6}$$

That is to say, let us assume that the social transformation function is independent of the distribution of wealth. Then, recalling equation (6) of the appendix to Chapter III, (5) yields

$$\frac{\partial T/\partial X_i}{\partial T/\partial X_j} = \frac{\partial B/\partial X_i}{\partial B/\partial X_j}. \qquad (i, j = 1, \ldots, n) \tag{7}$$

This means that the social production and Bergson frontiers must be tangential to one another at the optimum point—provided that it is not a boundary extremum (in which case the equations (3) themselves break down, as the functions are not ordinarily differentiable at such points); and provided that external effects in consumption are not excessive, in which case it gives a minimum, rather than a maximum, value of W.†

Note that the marginal social rates of indifference involved in equations (5) and (7) in general depend explicitly on the welfare function used. Interpersonal comparisons are therefore required to determine their sizes. Recalling our discussion of equation (7) of the appendix to Chapter III, however, it is clear that this is only the case when external effects exist in consumption. If we follow Pareto in assuming them away, the first-order conditions for the General Optimum are quite independent of interpersonal comparisons. We have

$$\frac{\partial T/\partial X_i}{\partial T/\partial X_j} = \frac{\partial u^1/\partial x_i^1}{\partial u^1/\partial x_j^1} = \cdot \cdot \cdot \cdot \cdot \cdot = \frac{\partial u^\nu/\partial x_i^\nu}{\partial u^\nu/\partial x_j^\nu}. \qquad (i, j = 1, \ldots, n) \tag{8}$$

† When external effects are excessive we have to write equation (2) as $T(x) \leq 0$. The inequality can only be dropped when we make the value judgement that a *cet. par.* increase in any output is desirable. This value judgement is not compatible with a Pareto W when external effects in consumption are excessive.

The second-order conditions, ensuring a regular maximum for W, could easily be set out. They add little, however, to the diagrammatic treatment used in the text; and so there is no point in pursuing the matter further.

THE WELFARE FRONTIER

The welfare frontier, or utility-possibility function, is a relation between the individual utility indicators of the form

$$P(u^1, \ldots, u^\nu) = 0, \tag{9}$$

which tells us the maximum value any one can attain (in view of the technological restraint imposed by the social transformation function), given the values of the remaining ones. We are chiefly interested in its construction and its slope.

It is convenient to start from the equations (3′). Multiplying by dx_i^α, summing over the i and the α, and taking account of equations (1) and (2), we have

$$\sum_\theta \lambda^\theta \, du^\theta = 0. \tag{10}$$

Whether or not this is an exact differential depends on whether or not integrability conditions analogous to those discussed in the appendix to Chapter II hold. Indeed, the whole discussion is along exactly the same lines. If the transformation and utility functions have a moderate degree of smoothness, there will exist a $P(u^1, \ldots, u^\nu)$ whose total differential is given by (10). Its slope in the (α, β)-plane is then

$$\frac{\partial u^\alpha}{\partial u^\beta} = -\frac{\partial P/\partial u^\beta}{\partial P/\partial u^\alpha} = -\frac{\lambda^\beta}{\lambda^\alpha}. \tag{11}$$

Now we have but to derive an expression for $\lambda^\beta/\lambda^\alpha$. This is most conveniently done by selecting a subset of ν of the $n\nu$ equations (3′), which are linear in the λ's. Let us select that subset involving derivatives with respect to x_s^α, $(\alpha = 1, \ldots, \nu)$. Adopting matrix notation, we have

$$[\partial u/\partial x_s]\,[\lambda] = -\mu'\,[\partial T/\partial x_s]. \tag{12}$$

When external effects do not exist in consumption, all the off-diagonal elements vanish in the matrix of (12), and it is completely straightforward to show that

$$\frac{\lambda^\beta}{\lambda^\alpha} = \frac{\partial u^\alpha/\partial x_s^\alpha}{\partial u^\beta/\partial x_s^\beta}\,\frac{\partial T/\partial x_s^\beta}{\partial T/\partial x_s^\alpha}. \tag{13}$$

Normally, the derivatives of the utility functions will be of the same sign—a good is likely to be a good, and a productive service a service, for all men in the community. Similarly, the derivatives of the transformation function with respect to x_s are likely to be of the same sign.

The ratio $\lambda^{\beta}/\lambda^{\alpha}$ will thus normally be positive, and the welfare frontier will normally slope downwards, whenever external effects are not present in consumption. In rare cases, however, the signs of $\partial T/\partial x_s^{\beta}$ and $\partial T/\partial x_s^{\alpha}$ may differ. Then the frontier will slope upwards. For the signs to differ it is necessary for the transformation function to depend on the distribution of wealth rather strongly and asymmetrically. Typically, a marginal transference of wealth from one man to another would, by itself (i.e. without there being any change in the number of hours worked), have to increase efficiency so much that output increased by more than the amount of the transfer.

The dependence of the social transformation function on the distribution of wealth is thus one source of an upward-sloping welfare frontier. Let us now examine the influence of external effects in consumption, abstracting from the dependence of the transformation function on the distribution of wealth. If we write A_s for the determinant of the matrix of (12), and A_s^{θ} for the determinant obtained by replacing each element in the θth column of A_s by unity, it is straightforward to show that

$$\frac{\lambda^{\beta}}{\lambda^{\alpha}}=\frac{A_s^{\beta}}{A_s^{\alpha}}. \qquad (\alpha, \beta=1, \ldots, \nu) \tag{14}$$

Inspection indicates that the presence of external effects can make A_s^{β}/A_s^{α} positive or negative, so that the frontier can slope either way.

In a two-person community, (14) gives a rather simple result. Recalling (11), we have

$$\frac{\partial u^{\alpha}}{\partial u^{\beta}}=-\frac{\dfrac{\partial u^{\alpha}}{\partial x_s^{\alpha}}-\dfrac{\partial u^{\alpha}}{\partial x_s^{\beta}}}{\dfrac{\partial u^{\beta}}{\partial x_s^{\beta}}-\dfrac{\partial u^{\beta}}{\partial x_s^{\beta}}}, \tag{15}$$

which shows that the frontier can slope upwards only when external economies (i.e. positive external effects) in consumption are marked and asymmetrical. That is to say: in a two-person community the absence of external economies in consumption is sufficient for a downward-sloping welfare frontier. In a larger community, however, this is not the case: the frontier can acquire a positive slope as a result of external diseconomies alone.

Note that, everywhere in the above discussion, the *sign* (but not the size) of the slope of the frontier is invariant under any arbitrary transformations of the utility indexes of the form $\phi(u)$, where $\phi'(u)>0$. This is important because, if we confine ourselves to Paretian welfare functions, positions in which the frontier slopes positively—in which we can make everybody better off—cannot be positions of maximum welfare.

CHAPTER V

FEASIBLE WELFARE

In the last chapter we discussed the 'potential desirability' of changes of two types. Firstly, those where we start from a position inside the welfare frontier, and move on to it, and secondly, those where we move from a position on one welfare frontier to a position on another. It is certain that only a few of the changes in which we are likely to be interested will fit into either of these categories. In general, we want to be able to say something about the potential desirability of changes which lead from a position inside one welfare frontier to a position inside another—or to another position inside the same frontier. We want to be able to compare sub-optimal situations.

THE EFFICIENCY LOCUS

Why do we want to be able to compare sub-optimal situations? Because it is, in the world about us, extraordinarily hard for a society to attain its welfare frontier. If external effects did not exist, if the production frontier were independent of the distribution of wealth, and if the relative curvature of the transformation and indifference curves were 'right', full competitive equilibrium might see it there—although there is no guarantee that it would unless we rule out the possibility of multiple equilibria. But, however favourable the circumstances and thoroughgoing the competition, full equilibrium is seldom attained. Moreover, the corrective taxes required whenever external effects do exist, or the relative curvature is 'wrong', are likely to be so exceedingly complicated that nothing better than the crudest approximations could be hoped for in practice. The same can be said of whatever corrective devices an enthusiast might succeed in inventing to allow for the dependence of the transformation functions on the distribution of wealth. In practice, therefore, it is probable that a society will find itself well within the frontier. Sub-optimal situations will usually be the only *feasible* ones.

Consider a point inside the welfare frontier whose co-ordinates represent the levels of well-being actually enjoyed by the various members of a community. A redistribution of wealth by lump-sum taxes and bounties (which are assumed to cost nothing to collect or distribute) will normally move society to another point within the frontier. The locus of all points traced out by redistributions of this kind we shall call the *efficiency locus*, because it depicts the allocative efficiency of an economy for various distributions of welfare.† Optimum allocative efficiency, for a particular distribution of welfare, is not attained unless the efficiency locus coincides with the welfare frontier in the point corresponding to that distribution.

It might be better to call the efficiency locus an 'actuality locus', since it always passes through the point where society actually is, and joins those to which it would actually be led by lump-sum redistributions. This would contrast suitably with the (usually unrealized) potentialities of the welfare frontier. But the idea of the allocative efficiency of an economy is an important one, and the term 'efficiency locus' serves to remind us of it.

It is perhaps most helpful to think of the relationship between the welfare frontier (or utility-possibility locus) and the efficiency locus in the following way. The welfare frontier shows the best we can do, given tastes and techniques, in an institutional vacuum. The efficiency locus shows the best we can do if we take the existing institutional set-up as a datum. It describes the result of distributional changes (by lump-sum measures) within that framework. This must not be interpreted too literally, however, for it is at least conceivable that institutional changes (in a more ordinary sense of the term) will accompany the lump-sum redistributions which move us from one part of an efficiency locus to another. Industries, cartels, trade unions, forms of market organization—these and others will come and go as the redistributions shift the pattern of demand. Moreover, it is not altogether obvious that such institutional changes (again in an ordinary sense of the term)

† By a 'distribution of welfare' is meant no more than a 'point in utility-space'—or, thinking of a two-person community, a 'point in the (α, β)-plane'.

would be reversible. If a great redistribution causes social revolution, so that factories and forests are razed to the ground, a restoration of the original distribution would not restore overnight the productive apparatus of society.

But the fact that movements along an efficiency locus may be irreversible is of little consequence. In any actual situation society will find itself in a particular position on the locus. Under certain circumstances it may be faced with a choice between remaining there and moving to another position on the locus. It is, generally speaking, a once-for-all change that is in question. Whether or not continuing to-and-fro movements can occur without changing the institutional set-up (and thus the locus itself) is largely irrelevant. The locus is defined by hypothetical lump-sum redistributions within the existing set-up at a given moment of time, not by a succession of redistributions through time. The observing economist is assumed to know the points to which they would lead. Any one of these points is attainable by making the appropriate redistribution; but they need not all be attainable in rapid succession.

THE FEASIBILITY LOCUS

These considerations have an important bearing on Professor Samuelson's view that lump-sum redistributions of wealth are impracticable.† In any modern society redistributions are made by altering the existing tax-structure, by rationing or by some other means which *would* affect the marginal equivalences of the General Optimum—that is, by measures which are *not* lump-sum. Income-taxes, for instance, clearly destroy the marginal equivalences, often rather vividly. Assume that a man is working up to the point at which his marginal physical product in terms of some numéraire (we shall call it his 'wage') is just sufficient to compensate him for his extra effort. This is one of the familiar equivalences of the General Optimum. Now let a tax on income be imposed. He will work up to the point at which his 'wage' *net of tax* is just sufficient to compensate for the extra effort. The General

† P. A. Samuelson, *Foundations of Economic Analysis* (Cambridge, Mass., 1947), pp. 247–8.

Optimum is destroyed—the social rate of indifference between rendering more of the productive service and consuming more of the product is no longer equal to the technological social rate at which the service can be transformed into the product at the margin. To be truly lump-sum a tax must bear no relation whatsoever to a man's effort or earnings. Or, more strictly, no man must anticipate that the tax he is to pay will bear any relation to his effort or earnings. Once imposed, it may cause him to work and earn either more or less; the size of the tax may affect the amount of effort forthcoming, but it must not be affected by it.

It is clear that truly lump-sum measures are extraordinarily hard to devise. A poll-tax, of course, meets all the requirements; but it is not very helpful in securing desired redistributions unless we tax different men differently. But on what criteria should we discriminate between different men? Ethical ones? And what if a man cannot pay the tax? If we start taxing the poor less than the rich, we are simply reintroducing an income-tax. If we tax able men more than dunderheads, we open the door to all forms of falsification: we make stupidity seem profitable—and any able man can make himself seem stupid. Unless we really do have an omniscient observing economist to judge men's capabilities, or a slave-market where the prices they fetch reflect expert appraisals of their capacities, any taxing authority is bound to be guided by elementary visible criteria like age, marital status and—above all—ability to pay. We are back with an income-tax.

This, I think, states fairly the case against the practicability of lump-sum redistributions. With it one can only agree. But it is still possible to argue that once-for-all redistributions can be achieved by lump-sum measures. It is only when we think in terms of a continuing process that they appear quite hopeless. Quite often, however, it seems that we have to think in terms of a continuing process; and then the efficiency locus loses much of its relevance. Let us take an example.

Consider a change which moves the efficiency locus. It will lead from a point on the 'old' locus to a point on the 'new' one, and may result in a distribution of welfare of which we not do approve.

Suitable lump-sum taxes and bounties can be imposed to 'correct' this unfavourable redistribution, penalizing those who have gained 'too much' and compensating those who have lost 'too heavily'. Such a correction is a clear-cut once-for-all measure. The efficiency locus is a useful tool for discussing the potential desirability of the original change. But if we consider a succession of such changes and a succession of corrective redistributions, the matter becomes more delicate. It is all too probable that the criteria on which the penalties and compensations (or taxes and bounties) are calculated will become known to the members of the community. If they discover these criteria—or come to think they have discovered them—they will suit their actions to them. If the losers by a change always seem to be compensated, and the gainers penalized (though not necessarily to the full extent of their loss or gain), it will be profitable to pretend that you have gained less, or lost more, than in fact you have. If the poor are compensated at the expense of the rich, it will be profitable to simulate a measure of poverty. But, falsification apart, the important thing is that incentives will be affected.† There will result a locus different from that which would obtain in the absence of such anticipatory behaviour. In other words, the 'lump-sum' taxes and bounties will no longer be truly lump-sum. They will affect our marginal equivalences, much as income-taxes would. When we think in terms of a sequence of changes, each one of which is accompanied by a corrective redistribution, the efficiency locus may cease to be a useful concept.

Whether we think in terms of a once-for-all redistribution or a continuing process will therefore determine whether we judge the potential desirability of a change with reference to the efficiency locus or what Professor Samuelson calls the *feasibility locus*.‡ The feasibility locus tells us how well off it is politically *feasible* to make any one man, given the levels of well-being enjoyed by the others. It does not necessarily take the existing institutional set-up as a datum, and movements along it are not secured by imposing

† Cf. A. C. Pigou, *The Economics of Welfare* (4th ed., London, 1932), Part IV, Chaps. IX and X.

‡ P. A. Samuelson, 'Evaluation of Real National Income', *Oxford Economic Papers*, New Series, vol. II (1950), pp. 18–19.

lump-sum measures. We move along it by whatever means are for the moment regarded as feasible, changing the institutional set-up as we go.

Through any point on a feasibility locus there passes an efficiency locus indicating the results of hypothetical lump-sum redistributions in the institutional environment corresponding to that point. We know that if we move along the feasibility locus as a result of a change involving something more than a mere lump-sum redistribution, we move from a point on one efficiency locus to a point on another. That is to say, the efficiency locus itself moves. But we can never be certain whether we have moved to a different point on the old feasibility locus, or to a point on a new one. We cannot be certain whether the feasibility locus has moved too until we know whether the change in question has affected the notion of political feasibility entertained. This seems to make the feasibility locus rather an awkward tool.

Indeed, the whole concept of political feasibility is itself so flexible that there is not much point in retaining the feasibility locus as a tool of analysis. Its introduction does serve to emphasize that a long series of lump-sum redistributional changes may be impracticable; but, once that has been grasped, we can afford to dispense with it. There is, however, a slightly different context in which the idea of feasibility can be quite helpful. Let us turn to it.

Fig. 13 illustrates the case—and, incidentally, also sums up the relationship between the three loci: utility-possibility (i.e. welfare frontier), efficiency, and feasibility. Society finds itself in *C*. Through that point both the efficiency locus, *EE*, and the feasibility locus, *FF*, must pass; but we can say little else about them except that they can never pass beyond the welfare frontier, or utility-possibility locus, *PP*. The *W* curves are social welfare contours. They indicate that welfare is higher in the 'sub-optimal' point *C* than in all points on the frontier, except those lying between *Q′* and *Q″*. Now if for some reason it is not feasible to attain the frontier between *Q′* and *Q″*—using 'feasible' in some broad and essentially arbitrary sense—we have a vague rationalization of the fact that society is at C, and not on the frontier. It is only vague, of course, because we have not ruled out the feasibility of approaching the frontier more closely than C; but that is easily remedied.

The rationing of common necessities in times of scarcity seems to provide a good example. Assume that, in the absence of rationing, society would be on its welfare frontier, but that the great scarcity of necessities entails a very 'unfavourable' distribution of welfare: the rich bid up the prices of the scarce goods to such an extent that the poor cannot buy enough to sustain life, even when they spend the whole of their incomes on them. A redistribution

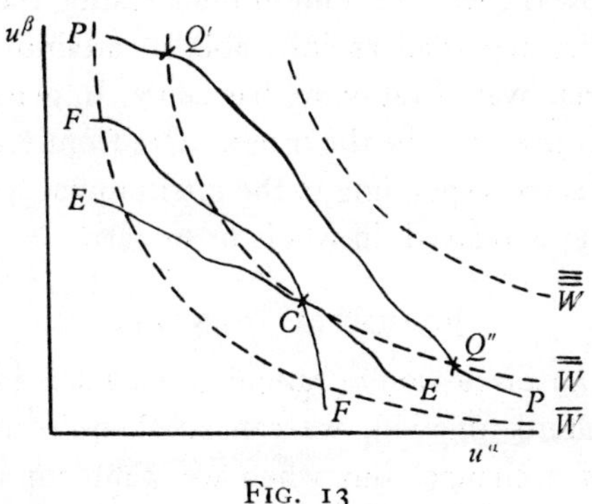

FIG. 13

of wealth could lead to a more favourable position on the frontier. But it may have to be a somewhat far-reaching redistribution; and, especially if the extreme scarcity is thought to be a transient affair, it may not be regarded as practicable. Temporary rationing may be a better alternative, even if it does distort the allocative efficiency of the economy by destroying the marginal equivalences which characterize the frontier.†

† Note that we started by assuming that society would be on the frontier in the absence of rationing. Professor Baumol has correctly pointed out that such an assumption may obscure one of the most interesting aspects of many rationing schemes—viz. that they are introduced because external effects in consumption suddenly become very marked in times of scarcity. The appeal of an 'equal shares for all' slogan provides an obvious example. It might therefore be more realistic to argue that the imposition of rationing, far from destroying the marginal equivalences of the General Optimum, actually leads (when we

The word 'temporary' should be emphasized. Elsewhere† I have argued that consumer rationing becomes less and less effective the longer it is kept in operation, unless it is buttressed by direct controls over the organization of production. (This is simply because rationing diverts expenditure to unrationed goods, and will, in the long run, tend to divert scarce factors of production to the industries producing them—and away from the industries where they are more urgently required.) The argument can be phrased in terms of the efficiency locus, or the point C in Fig. 13, drifting inwards with the passage of time and the diversion of resources to the production of less wanted goods. Eventually C will drop below the welfare contour demarcating the section of the welfare frontier regarded as infeasible of attainment. Then the time for the removal of rationing has come. In general, of course, PP in Fig. 13 need not be the true welfare frontier. It can be the efficiency locus corresponding to the institutional set-up obtaining when rationing is relaxed, in whole or in part.

POTENTIAL BENEFIT

When, as in our discussion of rationing, we make explicit use of a particular welfare function, we can speak quite directly of the desirability of a change. But when we want our conclusions to have greater generality, we must speak more circumspectly. In the last chapter we defined the 'potential desirability' of a change in terms which are valid for all Pareto W's—that is, without making any interpersonal comparisons of well-being. But our treatment was handicapped by the fact that we only had the welfare frontier at our disposal. It can only be applied to economies

take account of external effects) to a closer approach to the frontier. Cf. William J. Baumol, 'Relaying the Foundations', *Economica*, vol. XVI (1949), p. 166.

The methods devised by Rothbarth, Kaldor, Nicholson and the present writer for measuring the change in real income caused by the introduction of rationing all ignore external effects in consumption, and are valid only if their absence can be assumed. This limits their usefulness greatly. For a survey of the methods see J. de V. Graaff, 'Rothbarth's "Virtual Price System", and the Slutsky Equation', *Review of Economic Studies*, vol. XV (2) (1947–8), pp. 91–5. When writing this paper I was unaware of the probable importance of Professor Baumol's argument.

† J. de V. Graaff, 'Towards an Austerity Theory of Value', *South African Journal of Economics*, vol. XVI (1) (1948), pp. 35–50.

which are optimally organized. Now that we have a more general piece of apparatus in the efficiency locus (we shall not bother about the feasibility locus too), it is instructive to cover the ground once again.

Technological 'progress', or a change of some other kind, is likely to affect both the welfare frontier and the efficiency locus. It may shift one and twist † the other, or affect both in the same way. There are; in fact, nine different combinations to consider: any one of the three different types of movement (inward shift, outward shift, twist) of the frontier can be associated with any one of the three different types of movement of the efficiency locus. For instance, an invention which shifts the frontier outwards may confer on the innovators monopoly power so great that the efficiency locus is given a twist, or even shifted inwards.

The question therefore arises: to which locus (or frontier) should we refer in judging the potential desirability of a particular change? The answer, I think, depends upon the context. If we regard the institutional framework inherited by society as malleable and subject to extensive alteration at will, the welfare frontier is attainable and therefore relevant. If, however, we are prepared (for the purposes in hand) to take the existing institutional set-up as a datum, and examine particular changes within the framework it provides, the efficiency locus becomes relevant. The same holds when we are not prepared to 'accept' (in an approbatory sense) the institutions which exist, if we feel that there is but little chance of altering them in a way which would lead towards the frontier.

In any event, a change will lead from a point on one efficiency locus to a point on another. Its potential desirability should normally be judged on that basis. Then we can consider the further question of altering institutions in a way which will improve the allocative efficiency of the economy so as to make the efficiency locus approach closer to the frontier. Such an improvement is always at least potentially beneficial. But it cannot be

† The reader will recall that 'twist' and 'shift' are not used synonymously with 'rotation' and 'translation'. The characteristic of a twist is simply the intersection of the old and new loci.

taken for granted. Its achievement is a matter quite distinct from the potential desirability of the original change. Thus an invention which shifts the efficiency locus inwards should normally be regarded as potentially harmful, even if it shifts the frontier outwards. But it may well be that the same invention *plus* a vigorous trust-busting campaign would shift the locus outwards. In that case the invention *plus* the trust-busting, as opposed to the invention alone, is to be judged at least potentially beneficial. This would be true even if the invention were to involve an inward shift of the frontier—although, in the latter eventuality, it might be thought that the trust-busting without the invention would be potentially even more beneficial. This would not necessarily be correct, however, as the success of a given trust-busting campaign might not be altogether independent of the invention.

It must not be inferred from the preceding argument that 'trust-busting' is in fact likely to cause an outward shift of the efficiency locus. It is, in the absence of an omniscient observing economist, almost impossible to say how trust-busting or anything else will affect it. For instance, in a world innocent of external effects and all the other embarrassing complications which require corrections even in a perfectly competitive economy, it cannot be said that the elimination of monopoly in a particular industry will shift the efficiency locus uniformly outwards. It cannot even be said that it will shift it outwards in the neighbourhood of the relevant point. It can be said that the elimination of monopoly *in all industries simultaneously* will perform this feat, but that is rather different—and not very helpful.

Is the efficiency locus then a tool worth introducing? It seems that it is. It provides us with a useful means for analysing the various 'compensation tests' which have been used by different writers in the last decade. The tests in their turn can be regarded as tackling part at least of the problem of determining movements in the locus.

COMPENSATION TESTS

The compensation tests all spring from a desire to see what can be said about social welfare or 'real national income' (the difference may be important) without making interpersonal comparisons of well-being—or, in the case of one variant, without making *detailed* interpersonal comparisons. They have a common origin in Pareto's definition of an increase in social welfare—that at least one man must be better off and no one worse off—but they are extended to situations in which some people are made worse off. It is here that the possibility of compensation becomes relevant.

Let us consider a two-person community for simplicity—the method of reasoning is quite general. Let us assume that, where compensations are involved, they can be made by lump-sum measures, so that the efficiency locus is the tool to use. We shall, however, simply speak of 'the locus', so that the reader who is sceptical of their practicability can think in terms of a feasibility locus (if he can define 'feasibility' to his own satisfaction).† We could, of course, use the welfare frontier instead of the locus; but then we should have to confine ourselves to optimally organized environments. Most of the compensation theorists seem to intend their tests to have greater generality.‡

(1) It is instructive to start with Pareto's definition, where no compensation is involved. An increase in social welfare is defined as a movement to the north-east (strictly: northwards, eastwards or in any intermediate direction) on either of the diagrams which follow, like that from Q_1 to Q_2 in Fig. 14.

(2) In 1939 Mr Kaldor§ suggested what is in effect a simple extension of (1) as a definition of an increase in 'physical productivity' or 'aggregate real income'. If, in Fig. 14, we move from Q_1 to R, and the locus through R passes north-east of Q_1 (i.e. 'outside' Q_1), the gainer by the change can profitably compensate

† Thus Professor Reder does not confine compensations to those attainable by lump-sum measures. He says that 'a compensating tax may be any kind of tax whatever'. (M. W. Reder, *Studies in the Theory of Welfare Economics* (New York, 1947), p. 16 n.)

‡ The Hicks test described in (3) below was in effect proposed with reference to an exchange-economy welfare frontier (i.e. to redistributions of a fixed collection of goods). But from a production-economy viewpoint this is no more than an efficiency locus touching the true frontier in the point or points where the fixed collection of goods is an optimal collection.

§ N. Kaldor, 'Welfare Propositions and Interpersonal Comparisons of Utility', *Economic Journal*, vol. XLIX (1939), pp. 549–52.

the loser. This, it was suggested, enables us to say that 'real income' is greater in R than in Q_1.

(3) In 1940 Professor Hicks† used the reverse test for an increase in 'real social income'. If we move from Q_2 to R in Fig. 14, we see that the locus through R passes inside Q_2. That is to say: the gainer by the change is unable to compensate the loser and remain a gainer. This, it was suggested, enables us to say that 'social income' was greater in Q_2 than in R; or that it would be increased by moving from R to Q_2. Note that this is not the same as the Kaldor test. For Q_2 to be 'better' than R on the basis of the

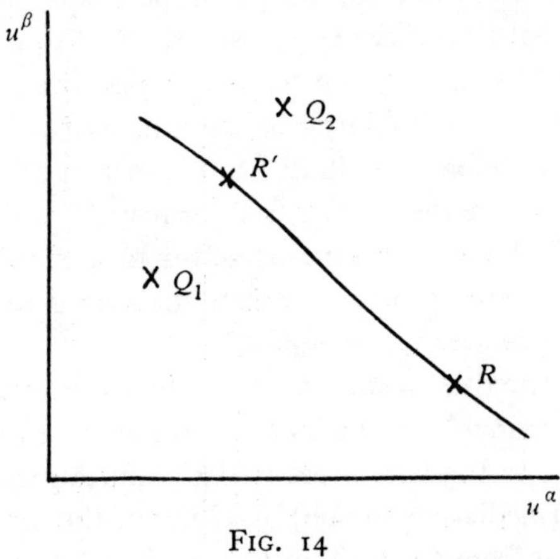

FIG. 14

Kaldor test it would be necessary for the locus through Q_2 to pass outside R. But we know nothing about the locus through Q_2. We are only told about the locus through R.

(4) Professor Scitovsky‡ was not long in demonstrating that, if compensation is not actually paid, the original Kaldor test (and, by implication, the Hicks one too) can lead to a contradiction.

† J. R. Hicks, 'The Valuation of Social Income', *Economica*, vol. VII (1940), pp. 105–24. In his *Studies in the Theory of Welfare Economics* (New York, 1947), Professor Reder does not distinguish between the Kaldor test (which uses the *status quo ante* as the base) and the Hicks one (which uses the *status quo post*).

‡ T. de Scitovsky, 'A Note on Welfare Propositions in Economics', *Review of Economic Studies*, vol. IX (1) (1941–2), pp. 77–88; cf. also *idem*, 'A Reconsideration of the Theory of Tariffs', *Review of Economic Studies*, vol. IX (2) (1942), pp. 89–110.

Let us consider again Q_1 in Fig. 14. The locus through R passes outside it, so R is 'better' than Q_1 on the Kaldor basis. But there is no reason why the locus through Q_1 should not pass outside R. If it does, we have, again on the Kaldor basis, Q_1 'better' than R. The two loci intersect and a contradiction emerges. Accordingly, Professor Scitovsky argued that we need a *double* test. Before we can say that 'welfare' (the use of the term is Professor Scitovsky's) increases when we move from Q_1 to R, we must know that the locus through R passes outside Q_1, *and* that the locus through Q_1 passes inside R. That is to say: the gainer by the change can

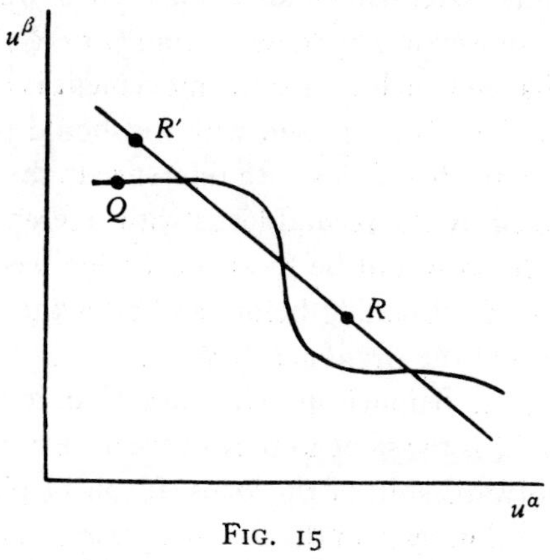

FIG. 15

profitably compensate the loser, or bribe him into accepting it; and the loser cannot profitably bribe the gainer into rejecting it.

(5) In 1947 Professor Samuelson† pointed out that even the Scitovsky test was unsatisfactory. What it does is to rule out the possibility of the loci intersecting (strictly: of their intersecting an odd number of times) between Q and R, but it does not rule out the possibility of their intersecting elsewhere (or of their intersecting an even number of times between Q and R). Fig. 15 illustrates the matter. The Scitovsky 'double test' is satisfied for a movement from Q to R. The gainer can profitably bribe the loser into

† P. A. Samuelson, *Foundations of Economic Analysis* (Cambridge, Mass., 1947), p. 251. Samuelson speaks in terms of the 'utility-possibility function', but there is no need to restrict his analysis to optimal environments.

accepting the movement; and the loser cannot profitably bribe the gainer into rejecting it. Yet the loci intersect several times. We cannot claim that there has been an *actual* increase in welfare in the strict Paretian sense, for one man is made worse off by the movement. And we cannot say that there has been a *potential* increase, for that requires—as we have seen—a shift, rather than a complicated twist, of the locus. Whether the highest position of social welfare is attained on the locus through Q or on that through R will clearly depend on the shape of our W contours—that is, on the ethical judgements we care to make.

Note that this statement holds good even if we experience an *actual* increase in welfare, by moving from Q to R'. We still cannot say that the change which causes the movement is even potentially beneficial. For there is no reason why we should judge the situation depicted by the first locus with reference to the single point Q, and that depicted by the second locus with reference to the single point R'. To do so would be to attach undue weight to the distribution of wealth obtaining before and after the change—to the *status quo ante* and the *status quo post*.

Accordingly, the Samuelson criterion for 'an increase in potential real income' † is the same as the one we have used for 'potential benefit': an outward shift of the locus. It can be phrased in terms of the compensation tests in the following way. For every possible distribution of wealth, both before and after the change in question occurs, the Kaldor and the Hicks tests (and therefore the Scitovsky double one) must be satisfied.

(6) Finally, Dr Little ‡ has suggested several variants of a rather different type of criterion—one which refers to an actual, not a potential, increase in real income or welfare (he uses the two terms synonymously). A typical variant is the following. Let us return to Fig. 14. A movement from Q_2 to R satisfies the Hicks test, since the locus through R passes inside Q_2. There must,

† The phrase is taken from P. A. Samuelson, 'Evaluation of Real National Income', *Oxford Economic Papers*, New Series, vol. II (1950), pp. 19–20.

‡ I. M. D. Little, 'The Foundations of Welfare Economics', *Oxford Economic Papers*, New Series, vol. I (1949), pp. 235–7; 'Welfare and Tariffs', *Review of Economic Studies*, vol. XVI (2) (1949–50), pp. 65–8; 'A Note on the Interpretation of Index Numbers', *Economica*, vol. XVI (1949), pp. 369–70.

therefore, exist a point on the locus, say R', in which everybody is worse off than in Q_2. Now if we are prepared to make the broad ethical judgement that R' is 'no worse' than R (in the sense that $W(R') \geqslant W(R)$), it follows that welfare must be higher in Q_2 than in R.

Note that we require, in addition to the information that the Hicks test is satisfied, the definite value judgement that $W(R') \geqslant W(R)$. This is a rather curious requirement. Why should we have to judge between R' and R in order to be able to say whether or not Q_2 is better than R? Why can't we judge between Q_2 and R quite directly? It seems fair to remark that the introduction of an intermediate point R' serves no useful purpose whatsoever.†

Summary. The reader is no doubt impressed by the diversity of the six tests; and he will have observed that they refer to quite different concepts. The Pareto and Little tests refer to 'actual welfare'; the Samuelson one to 'potential welfare' in the sense we have used the term in this and the preceding chapter; the Kaldor and Hicks ones to 'real income'. Professor Scitovsky says his refers to 'social welfare', but that is difficult to concede—it would be more correct to say that it refers to potential welfare, and that on the basis of the *status quo ante* and *status quo post* only. It is valid if, and only if, we are prepared to accept one or both of these questionable bases.

There is, moreover, a considerable difference in the meanings attached to 'real income' in the Kaldor and the Hicks tests. Professor Hicks gives it a definite welfare connotation, which would be legitimate only if the compensation were actually paid. Then everybody would be better off and the Pareto test would tell us that 'actual welfare' had increased. Mr Kaldor uses 'real income' to mean the 'production of wealth', which he distinguishes from its 'distribution'. 'Welfare' depends on them both. An analysis

† It may even be a hindrance. When, as in the third of his cited papers (above, p. 88 n.), Dr Little applies his criterion to changes in the national income between one year and another, we actually experience both Q_2 and R. It may therefore be possible to judge between them. But we do not experience R' at all, and may not have much idea of what it would be like if experienced.

of this attempted dichotomy is reserved for the next section. Here it is sufficient to note that, if the compensation were actually paid, the Kaldor test, like the Hicks one, would reduce to Pareto's—and would begin to refer to 'actual welfare' instead of 'production'.

When compensation is not actually paid, the Kaldor and the Hicks tests become rather difficult to interpret positively, but they do provide us with a piece of negative information for which we should be grateful. *If 'Q is better than R' in either the Kaldor or the Hicks sense, we know that R cannot be potentially better than Q in the full Samuelson sense—which is the only satisfactory one.*

There is an aspect of the Pareto and Little criteria which requires emphasis. They are merely intended to refer to two *points* in the diagrams—not to the *whole range* of positions on the two loci passing through the points. They refer to actual situations, not to hypothetical ones resulting from hypothetical redistributions of wealth. That is what is meant by saying that they refer to actual, rather than potential, welfare. If, for example, an invention increases actual welfare in this sense, it does not follow that its introduction is 'potentially beneficial'. Actual welfare might be increased still more by redistributing wealth in the absence of the invention.

SIZE AND DISTRIBUTION

In putting forward and, later, in defending† his test, Mr Kaldor follows common practice in drawing a sharp distinction between a change in 'production' and a change in 'the distribution of wealth'. The latter, he freely admits, cannot be judged without introducing ethical valuations or 'political postulates'. But whether production increases or decreases can be judged, he would argue, by a compensation test. If the gainers can compensate the losers, it has increased.‡ Whether or not we say that welfare has increased too depends on our valuation of the way in which the

† N. Kaldor, 'A Comment' on W. J. Baumol's 'Community Indifference', *Review of Economic Studies*, vol. XIV (1) (1946–7), p. 49.

‡ In the paper just cited Mr Kaldor accepts the Scitovsky criticism that, to be free from inconsistency, the test must be a double one—i.e. that both the Kaldor and the Hicks tests must be satisfied.

'increased production' is distributed. Ethics are involved in talking about 'distribution', but not in talking about 'production'. The two can and should be separated. This is Mr Kaldor's view, shared by many. Indeed, a dichotomy between production and distribution is characteristic of the writings of a large majority of welfare economists. It appears in the classical Pigovian distinction between the size and the distribution of the national dividend. Yet it seems to be quite untenable if an individualist approach to social welfare is to be maintained (and it would appear to be the assumption of all the compensation theorists that it is). Let us see why this is so.

In a one-commodity world some definite meaning could be attached to a phrase like 'the size of the national income'; and we could legitimately say that welfare depended upon the size and the distribution of the output of this one commodity. But as soon as we leave a one-commodity world this ceases to be true. There is no unambiguous meaning which we can attach to 'the size of the national income' when we have a heterogeneous collection of goods and services. How can we combine the various goods into a single quantity which can be said to have a 'size'? By weighting them and striking an average? This is certainly a possibility. But we can only get the relevant weights from a welfare function; and, if we have the usual Paretian one of the form $W(u^1, \ldots, u^\nu)$, it will only tell us what weights to use when the distribution of the goods among the members of the community is given. Only in a very limited sense can welfare be said to depend on 'size' and 'distribution'—for the two elements are no longer independent, and cannot be separated out.

Mr Kaldor's way of trying to avoid the difficulty amounts to saying that 'size' or 'production' is constant, while distribution varies, along any efficiency locus. This would be perfectly satisfactory if we could guarantee that no two efficiency loci ever intersected. Then higher loci would represent greater, and lower ones smaller, production. But when we cannot guarantee that they never intersect, the distinction becomes blurred, and the dichotomy between production and distribution untenable.

It may be helpful to set out the argument symbolically. We have a heterogeneous collection of goods and services whose aggregate amounts can be written $\{X_1, \ldots, X_n\}$. We have also a social welfare function, $W(u^1, \ldots, u^\nu)$. In it the individual utility indicators depend not on the aggregate amounts $\{X_1, \ldots, X_n\}$, but on the amounts of particular goods and services going to particular members of the community. Now, clearly, it is very seldom that we can rewrite W as a function like $W^*(X_1, \ldots, X_n; \delta)$, where δ is some index of distribution. For W is a function of ν independent variables, whereas W^* would be a function of $(n+1)$. We cannot simply change from the one to the other. If we try to we must expect contradictions to arise. As we have seen, the expectation is not disappointed.

Another way of putting the matter is to say that the size-distribution dichotomy is inconsistent with the basic Paretian value judgements that individual preferences are to count and that a *cet. par.* increase in any one man's well-being increases social well-being. A satisfactory theory of welfare based on these judgements must, therefore, dispense with the time-honoured device of drawing a distinction between the size and the distribution of the national income and saying that welfare depends upon them both. It depends (if we must use the term) on size only—and we do not know what the size is until we know the distribution. Moreover, 'size' in this sense will generally change whenever the distribution changes, even if the collection of goods and services distributed remains the same.

To this matter we return in Chapter XI. There we shall explore some of the consequences of dropping the Paretian value judgements so as to be able to maintain the size-distribution dichotomy —which, apart from being of great practical convenience, seems to provide a possible rationalization for the conventional valuations of social income.

CHAPTER VI

INVESTMENT AND THE HORIZON

The preceding chapters were explicitly based on three important simplifying assumptions: (i) that the time horizon and the terminal capital equipment are somehow given; (ii) that inputs and outputs are perfectly divisible; and (iii) that there is no uncertainty. In this chapter, and the two that follow, we shall proceed to relax these assumptions, one at a time. As we do so we shall find many familiar conclusions crumbling about us; but that is the price we have to pay for approaching closer to reality.

CHOICE OF A HORIZON

The choice of a time-horizon is of prime importance. It demarcates the group whose welfare it is the purpose of all our analysis to maximize. If the horizon is set at the year 2000, it is the men now living and the men to be born before the turn of the century—the observing economist is assumed to know who they are—who will constitute the group. Their tastes will provide the standards of reference against which we judge the potential desirability of various changes; and it is between them that we may be called upon to make interpersonal comparisons of well-being.

It is clear that whether we set the horizon next year or next century is generally going to make a considerable difference to our attitude towards a particular change. Or, more strictly, it is going to make a considerable difference unless we accept a value judgement to the effect that the preferences of our contemporaries are to be given great weight, and those of unborn generations negligible weight, in the formation of our attitudes. Since many people might be prepared to accept a value judgement of this sort, it is worth seeing where it would lead us.

Let us number men in the order in which they were, or are to be, born; and let us assume as usual that we are only concerned with Paretian welfare functions—those which let a *cet. par.* increase in any one man's welfare increase social welfare. We can write the typical Paretian function as $W(u^1, \ldots, u^\nu)$, where u^ν is the utility indicator of the last man to be born before the horizon is attained. Now if the value judgements or ethical beliefs expressed by W are such that it responds very sensitively to changes in the earlier u's, but hardly at all to changes in the later u's, it seems probable that it will not matter very much if we 'truncate' W a little by omitting some of the later ones and bringing the horizon closer to hand. That is to say: it seems probable that, on the basis of a broad and simple value judgement (to the effect that the well-being of the present generation is much more important than the well-being of future generations), the precise location of the horizon will not be of great consequence.

At first sight this conclusion may appear quite encouraging. It may be thought that a value judgement of the sort required would find fairly wide acceptance—at least among the members of the present generation, and especially if we take account of the fact that they (as opposed to the omniscient observing economist) are certain to have no more than a very hazy notion of what the tastes of future generations are likely to be. But I doubt if the conclusion is as satisfactory as at first appears. However plausible it may seem to attribute little weight to individual u's belonging to men yet to be born, an extraordinarily strong value judgement is required to attribute little weight to their collective influence. The further ahead we look, the more insignificant becomes the place of our contemporaries in relation to that of the never-ending succession of future generations. Unless we firmly believe the Day of Judgement to be just around the corner, the mere weight of their numbers may win in the long run.

But what happens if we allow for uncertainty? The conventional theory of the firm suggests that it might help to solve the problem. There is for the firm (as opposed to the consumer, who has his allotted threescore years and ten) no natural span of life over which its profits (or utility) are to be maximized.† Consequently,

† There is a natural span if we assume that, instead of the firm maximizing profits, the entrepreneur maximizes utility. Even if the maximizing period is the same in both cases, the two assumptions do not give the same results unless the entrepreneur's own services to his firm are priced on the market. If he renders

we have either to assume some arbitrary 'profit-maximizing period' or to invoke the aid of uncertainty. If we adopt the latter course (which is the sensible one) we can assume that the firm seeks to maximize the present value of its expected stream of profits, and that as the stream recedes into the mists of the future it is more and more heavily discounted for uncertainty. The precise length of the stream is then of little consequence.† Could we not, by invoking uncertainty, say that the precise location of the horizon is of little consequence in welfare theory? Perhaps we could. The reader may prefer to suspend judgement until he has read Chapter VIII. But it is very doubtful if such a solution would be satisfactory. Not only may different men discount for uncertainty in different ways, and thus have different ideas about the (effective) length of the stream, but our standards of reference (individual preference-scales) become more uncertain too. In solving one problem we land ourselves with worse ones.

There is, however, not much point in discussing the matter further. The plain fact is that a definite value judgement is

a service which is not priced, it cannot be added into money cost. In these circumstances maximizing utility (which is affected by the amount of the 'private factor' rendered) will, in general, lead to behaviour different from that which the quest for money profits would entail.

It is quite simple to show that, when a price-change occurs, the existence of private factors of this sort will lead to 'income effects' in the theory of the firm analogous to those encountered in the theory of consumer behaviour. Even under pure competition, these can give rise to backward-rising supply curves from firms, and to positively-sloped demand curves for factors of production (so that a rise in wages may increase the employment of labour in a particular firm, even although the prices of all other inputs and outputs are held constant). Moreover, they can be shown to result in additional chances of instability in a General Equilibrium System—not only because of the 'income effects' in production, but also because the 'substitution effects' of a price-change become much less well-behaved.

Some of these problems have been touched upon by T. de Scitovsky, 'A Note on Profit Maximization and its Implications', *Review of Economic Studies*, vol. XI (1943), pp. 57–60, and M. W. Reder, 'A Reconsideration of Marginal Productivity Theory', *Journal of Political Economy*, vol. LV (1947), pp. 450–8; but the whole matter requires definitive treatment.

† This is, of course, true only within limits. A good deal of the recent controversy on the theory of the firm may be explicable in terms of differing views about the (effective) length of the profit-stream. Thus the ideas expressed by Mr Andrews can be interpreted as meaning that most firms take a longer view than is conventionally assumed. In this longer period the demand curves for their products are naturally more elastic, and competition more perfect, than might appear at first sight. Cf. P. W. S. Andrews, *Manufacturing Business* (London, 1949).

required to determine the location of the horizon, and it matters but little whether it takes the form of an outright decision, a heavy discrimination against the later *u*'s in *W*, or a convention on the way in which it is 'proper' to discount for uncertainty. It is a value judgement which each man must make for himself. One, looking a certain distance ahead, may favour a change which in his view will make every member of society better off; another, looking still further ahead, may regard the same change with disfavour, fearing that it will harm his children or his children's children. The 'groups' whose welfare the two men are estimating are not the same. There is no reason why their estimates should coincide.

Very occasionally there may be unanimity on the location of the horizon. Then we can claim that our welfare theory has a true individualist basis. But if there is not unanimity, or only unanimity within a certain group, we have in effect a paternalist element at the very foundation of our theory. For to say anything at all about welfare on an individualist basis we must demarcate the group of individuals in which we are interested; to demarcate the group we must fix the horizon; and the horizon fixed must, so to speak, be paternalistically imposed on all who do not happen to share our view of its 'proper' location. It is important to bear this in mind when evaluating the claim that welfare economics can be satisfactorily based on individual preferences.

It is sometimes suggested that a way of avoiding the necessity of having to fix a horizon can be found by passing the responsibility on to the household, where paternalist elements properly belong. We can—so the suggestion runs—concentrate on contemporary households and let them do the looking ahead and the providing for posterity. It seems that this position is untenable; but before seeing why, it is convenient to dispose of one or two other matters.

TERMINAL CAPITAL EQUIPMENT

Terminal capital equipment is the capital equipment (including inventories) left over when the horizon is attained. Hitherto we have just supposed that its amount is somehow 'given'; but now we must inquire how, or by whom, it is to be 'given'. There seem to be three approaches to the problem:

(1) We can take the view that the group demarcated by the horizon really is (in a very strict sense) the only one in whose welfare we are interested. Then it is reasonable to suppose that terminal capital equipment will be zero. Maximization of the welfare of a group over a given period of time implies, in strictness, the utter exhaustion of all physical capital by the end of that period.

But it seems probable that this interpretation of the horizon would be too strict for most people. Even the staunchest individualist might prefer to regard it as the point in time *beyond which individual preferences are no longer to be taken into account.* Beyond the horizon, he might say, too little is known about them to make it worth while trying to take them into consideration; but some provision must be made, and this can best be done by seeing that terminal capital equipment is not zero—by leaving mines and minerals, factories and forests, reasonably intact. Posterity should not be expected to start from scratch. Unless it is firmly believed that the Day of Judgement will coincide with the horizon, terminal equipment should be positive.

(2) If these value judgements are accepted, one way of giving them effect is to assume that items of terminal capital equipment enter directly into the preference-scales of some or all members of the community. Then their optimal 'outputs' are determined (in exactly the same way as the optimal outputs of ordinary collective goods) by the marginal equivalences of the General Optimum.

Whether or not this is, on empirical grounds, a reasonable assumption to make, cannot be settled here. But, if it is made, one important implication must be stressed. One's preference for a piece of machinery (or terminal capital equipment) depends essentially upon the future flow of final consumers' goods towards which it is expected to contribute. As techniques change, or as the organization of production changes, so too will one's preference change. That is to say: it may not be possible to assume constancy of tastes when an invention occurs, or when monopoly is eliminated in a particular industry. It may not be possible to move about inside the welfare frontier without causing the frontier itself to move.

It is most important to note this point. Our whole discussion of the General Optimum was explicitly based on the assumption that terminal capital equipment was 'given'. On that basis it was possible to take tastes as constant and deduce all the conventional marginal equivalences as necessary conditions for maximum welfare. The analysis depended on a very strict adherence to the assumption that an individual man's well-being was determined by the goods and services he and others consumed, the productive services he and others rendered, and nothing else. When we let items of terminal capital equipment affect his well-being, the whole analysis breaks down. For anything which affects the productivity of capital must then have a direct and independent effect (i.e. one which does not operate through changes in the quantities of goods consumed and services rendered) on his well-being. The organization of production, the institutional framework of society, the occurrence of an invention—all these are in that category. The conventional marginal equivalences of the General Optimum cannot be deduced if such variables are included in the individual utility functions.

(3) Unless we take the view of the horizon discussed in (1), and let terminal capital equipment be zero, we cannot claim simultaneously that the marginal equivalences of the General Optimum are necessary conditions for maximum welfare *and* that the amounts of the various items of terminal equipment are determined in accordance with individual preferences. If we want the marginal equivalences to stand, we must let them be determined independently of individual preference—i.e. *paternalistically*. As in Chapter IV, we must assume that they are given and fixed. This is the third approach to the problem.

We should, however, bear one point in mind before admitting another paternalist element at the very foundation of our theory (the determination of the horizon is one which is probably already there). The appeal of the thoroughgoing individualist approach is that it is based on a very few ethical propositions which are of such a sort that they are likely to command wide acceptance. (In brief, it is based on the familiar ethical propositions which characterize all Paretian welfare functions: that individual preferences are to 'count' and that a *cet. par.* increase in any one man's welfare increases social welfare.) It is based, that is to say, so broadly that people who hold widely divergent views on a number (or even the majority) of subjects are likely to accept it as a starting-point—at least, that is what its proponents appear to contend. But once we recognize that, in addition to agreeing on the location of the horizon, people would have to agree on the whole list of items of terminal capital equipment—a list which is likely to be extremely long and detailed—the contention loses much of its force. Many who agree on the broad Paretian ethical propositions will disagree deeply on such specific matters as these. There is thus no reason why their opinions regarding the desirability, or potential desirability, of a particular change should coincide. Interpersonal comparisons of some sort are required if a balance is to be struck.

THE 'POLITICAL' NATURE OF INVESTMENT

The rate of investment in any society determines what can be called the intertemporal distribution of welfare. Its optimum rate therefore depends on the extent to which we think it desirable to sacrifice present welfare for the benefit of posterity. It depends, that is to say, on the particular welfare function we employ.

This may be all that certain writers have in mind when they claim that the optimum rate of investment is essentially a 'political' matter†—in the same way that the distribution of wealth among contemporaries is sometimes called a political matter. It does not, however, appear to be what Professor Lerner has in mind when

† A. P. Lerner, *The Economics of Control* (New York, 1944), p. 262. Cf. also F. J. Atkinson, 'Saving and Investment in a Socialist State', *Review of Economic Studies*, vol. xv (2) (1947–8), pp. 78–83 and the references there cited. (Atkinson takes the opposite view.)

arguing the point, as his general position seems to be to deny that the distribution of wealth is political†; and it by no means goes to the heart of the problem. There are several distinct steps in determining the optimum rate of investment. First, we must choose the horizon and the amounts of the various items of terminal capital equipment. Once this choice has been made, we must secure the satisfaction of the marginal equivalences of the General Optimum. Their satisfaction will lead us to the welfare frontier, and in that sense determine the optimum rate of investment this side of the horizon.‡ But we are not home yet. The point on the welfare frontier to which we are led may not be the one we desire —it may represent 'too much' or 'too little' provision for our children. By means of lump-sum redistributions of wealth§ we can move along the frontier to the point we desire. The rate of investment will generally change as we go.

The only step in this process which could be called 'non-political' (in the loose sense that, since everyone could benefit, no one should dispute) is the attainment of the frontier. Whether we call the other steps 'political', 'paternalist' (because, in the absence of unanimity, we have to override individual preferences), or anything else, is largely a matter of taste. The important thing

† Lerner, *op. cit.* Chap. III. Arguing from the premisses that different people enjoy similar satisfactions and that the marginal utility of income diminishes, Lerner reaches the conclusion that 'probable satisfaction' is maximized by the equal division of income among the members of the community. His concept of social welfare thus differs from ours in that it is based on the sum of cardinally measurable individual satisfactions, and not on observable choices. But, accepting this, the 'equal ignorance' assumption involved is extremely unsatisfactory. If we do not know what people's capacities for satisfaction are, we simply do not know. There is no justification for assuming them equal. From absolute ignorance we can derive nothing but absolute ignorance.

‡ Dr Lange is clearly claiming too much when he states, without reservation, that the satisfaction of the marginal equivalences of the General Optimum implicitly determines the optimum rate of capital formation. Cf. Oscar Lange, 'The Foundations of Welfare Economics', *Econometrica*, vol. X (1942), p. 226.

§ Strictly, 'intertemporal lump-sum redistributions'. I do not wish to go in detail into the question of how these are best secured. It is probably easiest to think of one in favour of posterity as an increase in government investment financed by lump-sum taxes on contemporaries, and of one against posterity as a decrease in investment accompanied by lump-sum bounties. Since (by assumption) we start on the welfare frontier, we have full employment. The taxes and bounties should therefore be just sufficient (in the aggregate) to maintain it when the rate of investment is varied.

about the optimum rate of investment is the very close connection it bears to the specific decisions we make regarding the horizon and the terminal capital equipment. If we decide to exhaust physical capital by the turn of the century, the optimum rate of investment over the intervening years may well be zero; if we plan to leave posterity well provided for, it may be very great. It is thus intimately dependent on decisions which, we have argued, it is extraordinarily hard to make on the basis of individual preferences.

With one exception, which we shall consider in a moment, something of this sort seems to be generally conceded nowadays.† But several writers ‡ have taken as their starting-point the Pigovian assertion that individual preferences *ought not* to count where decisions affecting the future are concerned, since individual men lack a 'telescopic faculty' and tend to underestimate future satisfactions.§ This is an entirely different argument. Throughout we have been assuming that individual preferences *do* count (i.e. we have been confining ourselves to Pareto *W*'s). Whether or not they *should* count is another matter. The point we have developed is that they *cannot*, in general, be used for determining the horizon; and that if they are used for determining terminal capital equipment the conventional marginal equivalences of the General Optimum are no longer necessary conditions for maximum welfare.

The exception to which we have referred is the following. It may appear that we can avoid all the difficulties associated with terminal capital equipment and the horizon by concentrating attention on contemporary households and letting them decide how

† Few economists since F. P. Ramsey have argued, on the basis of utility theory, that there is any such thing as *the* optimum rate of investment. (Cf. F. P. Ramsey, 'A Mathematical Theory of Saving', *Economic Journal*, vol. XXXVIII (1928), pp. 543–59.) As recently as 1945, however, Professor Meade took Lerner to task for not considering the Ramsey argument. This is rather surprising, as the crudity of the assumptions Ramsey was forced to make to get a solution is apt to jar the modern reader somewhat. (Cf. J. E. Meade, 'Mr Lerner on "The Economics of Control"', *Economic Journal*, vol. IV (1945), pp. 47–69.)

‡ Cf. especially M. Dobb, *Political Economy and Capitalism* (New York, 1940), pp. 295 ff.

§ A. C. Pigou, *The Economics of Welfare* (4th ed., London, 1932), p. 25. Just how one could ever hope to establish whether or not men had a 'telescopic faculty' is by no means clear. Cf. the discussion of time-preference in Chapter III.

much to save. The most refiined version of the theory has recently been put forward by Mr Atkinson.† We can formulate it in these terms:

Let us assume tnat an approved distribution of wealth between households is maintained, and that the state adjusts the supply of money so as to secure that rate of interest which stimulates just sufficient investment to maintain the desired (or full-employment) level of income. This rate of investment, it is argued, is the optimum one.

There are several flaws in this reasoning. It is convenient to discuss first one which should, in strictness, be reserved for the chapter on Uncertainty.‡ We have the outputs of all goods and services determined by the marginal equivalences of the General Optimum, and the 'output' (or quantity) of money determined by the condition that it depresses the rate of interest just sufficiently to secure full employment. But what determines the volume (or 'nominal value') of bonds?§ Clearly, the matter is not unimportant. One volume of bonds will require one quantity of money to depress the rate of interest to the full-employment level; another volume, another quantity of money. But there is no guarantee that the full-employment rate of interest will remain unchanged. The amount people save out of a given income at a particular rate of interest is not independent of the form in which they can hold their assets (e.g. bonds of various maturities, and cash). We must recognize that the full-employment level of saving, and therefore of invest-

† F. J. Atkinson, 'Saving and Investment in a Socialist State', *Review of Economic Studies*, vol. xv (2) (1947–8), pp. 78–83. It should be emphasized that Atkinson talks of 'individuals' rather than 'households'. I have rephrased the argument in terms of the latter so as to connect up with the 'household solution' of the 'horizon problem' referred to in concluding the section on the Choice of a Horizon.

‡ We cannot discuss the motives for holding money unless we are prepared to admit uncertainty. It is doubtful if true money (which yielded no direct utility) would exist in a certain world. Cf. F. H. Knight, *Risk, Uncertainty and Profit*, p. xxii of Preface to L.S.E. reissue (London, 1933).

I purposely ignore the familiar arguments that no investment at all may be undertaken at any positive rate of interest, or that the rate of interest may hang by its bootstraps at a level too high for investment to reach the full employment volume. They are, however, clearly relevant.

§ 'Bonds' is used to cover all paper titles to wealth. In a socialist state of the sort Mr Atkinson considers, these may be restricted to government securities; but the argument is quite general.

ment, is arbitrary until the volume of bonds—and their pattern of maturities—is given.

Ignoring this point, however, the reasoning is still faulty. Let us abstract from such familiar difficulties as external effects in production and consumption, the dependence of the production functions on the distribution of wealth, or the presence of monopoly. Let us assume, that is to say, conditions completely favourable to the satisfactory working of the price mechanism. The amount of saving any one household undertakes (out of a given income, and at a given rate of interest) will depend upon the goods and services it expects those savings to be able to purchase in future years—upon the expected levels of prices. If it holds a part of its savings in the form of bonds, expected interest rates will enter the picture; if in the form of money, the general level of prices; if in the form of durable commodities, relative prices. But the prices which will actually prevail in the future depend upon the savings decisions of other households, now and in the future. This is so, not only on the demand side, but also because the savings decisions of all households together determine the rate of capital formation—and thus the future supply of goods and services. No one household has any way of knowing what other households intend to do. The market does not provide it with the information it requires to make a rational decision.

This is perhaps one of the more important senses in which the rate of saving (and investment) is unavoidably 'political'. The ordinary mechanism of the market cannot handle it. The ballot-box, or something else, must be substituted for the price system.

It is worth noting that this would not be the case if we had perfect forward markets for all commodities, extending indefinitely into the future. But we are never likely to be so fortunate; and, in their absence, we have each household trying to decide how much to save in monetary terms without knowing what the real value of its savings will be in the future. The dependence of their real value on the present and future savings of other households is analogous to external effects in consumption—but is quite distinct from them, as it works through the price system and has nothing to do with the interrelation of utilities. Like true external effects, however, it leads (from a welfare point of view) to a breakdown in the ordinary price mechanism.

When we discussed in Chapter IV the conditions under which perfect competition would lead to the satisfaction of the marginal equivalences of the General Optimum, we implicitly assumed the existence of perfect forward markets. Competition was assumed to be perfect in the strictest possible sense—through time as well as at any moment of time. In Chapter IV we deliberately slurred over this assumption, to concentrate attention on the cases where—in spite of it—the marginal equivalences would not be realized. It is not very surprising that its relaxation leads to further cases where they would not be realized. Household saving provides one example. Investment by individual entrepreneurs provides another.

No individual entrepreneur can estimate, on the basis of market data alone, the productivity of investment until the investment plans of other entrepreneurs are determined.† How can one say what the productivity of investment in a particular town will be until one knows whether or not that new railway line is to be laid down? ‡ We have here something analogous to external effects in production—but again it is something quite distinct from true external effects, since it works through the price system and has nothing to do with the interrelation of production functions in a technological sense. It nevertheless leads to a similar breakdown in the ordinary price mechanism.

Thus there is yet another sense in which the determination of the rate of investment is unavoidably 'political'. If it were all undertaken by the state, or by a single entrepreneur, the difficulty would be met. But to meet the corresponding difficulty on the consumption side we should have to let all savings decisions be undertaken by the state—or by a single household (which would then know how much other households were going to save—viz. zero).

† A full discussion of these and related matters is contained in W. J. Baumol, *Welfare Economics and the Theory of the State* (London, 1952).

‡ Cf. L. M. Lachmann, 'Investment Repercussions', *Quarterly Journal of Economics*, vol. LXII (1948), pp. 698–713.

This is a far cry from letting each household make its own decisions. Moreover, the difficulties on the consumption and investment sides must be met simultaneously. It is no use letting the state decide how much to save if it does not know what the pattern of investment, and therefore the real value of its savings, is to be.

We can safely conclude that no real solution of the problems we have been discussing in this chapter is to be found in concentrating on contemporary households, and letting them decide how far to look ahead and how much to provide for posterity. These are not decisions which households, acting separately, are equipped to make. There is no satisfactory 'competitive solution' to the problems of the horizon and terminal capital equipment or of investment generally. Households must act collectively—if they are to act at all. And, in the absence of unanimity, the decisions they make must be imposed on those who disagree with them. Politics—or paternalism—is involved.

CHAPTER VII

INDIVISIBILITY

Indivisibility creates no problems whatever if we actually have a well-defined social welfare function, W, with which to work. We can compare welfare in any two situations by direct substitution of the values of the relevant variables in it, whether or not those variables can vary continuously. The problems only arise when we do not have a definite W, but try to see how much we can say that will be true for a wide class of functions.

In the preceding chapters we confined ourselves to welfare functions of the Paretian type, and saw that it was possible to state various conditions—the marginal equivalences of the General Optimum—which must necessarily hold whenever any one of them attains a maximum (unless external effects in consumption are excessive). These conditions thus possess great generality, and are of interest to anyone who accepts the broad value judgements characterizing Paretian welfare functions—that individual preferences are to 'count' and that a *cet. par.* increase in any one man's welfare increases social welfare. Unfortunately, however, the marginal equivalences of the General Optimum are only valid necessary conditions for maximum welfare if perfect divisibility is assumed. If it is not, they break down.

I say that this is unfortunate because the marginal equivalences of the General Optimum are virtually the *only* things anyone has succeeded in discovering which are true for a wide range of welfare functions. That, coupled with the fact that under favourable circumstances they might be satisfied in a competitive environment, has led to enormous emphasis being placed upon them. They have, indeed, become the very stuff of welfare economics, as generally taught in the textbooks; † and have even tended to assume an

† Cf. M. W. Reder, *Studies in the Theory of Welfare Economics* (New York, 1947), Chaps. II ff. A. P. Lerner, *The Economics of Control* (New York, 1944), *passim*.

importance in their own right. 'Pricing principles' for state enterprises have been based upon them, and much reformist zeal has been devoted to devising institutional frameworks within which they would flourish. The writings of some economists seem to portray a belief that the 'problems of planning' and the 'economics of socialism' consist of little else.

It is therefore important to get a proper sense of proportion and to realize that they are no more than necessary conditions for maximum welfare under certain rather restrictive assumptions, one of which is that all goods and services are perfectly divisible. They are not sufficient conditions; indeed, they are not always even a complete set of necessary ones. For instance, when there are no external effects in consumption, they may lead to a position on the welfare frontier, but they will not select the most favoured point on the frontier—where a contour of the social welfare function just touches it (cf. Fig. 9; this tangency would complete the set of necessary conditions).† And many points where they are not satisfied will represent greater social welfare than many points where they are—that is, many points off the frontier will lie on higher social welfare contours than many points on it. If we do not have the distribution of wealth we want, we may do well to sacrifice the equality of marginal rates of transformation and indifference.

But the marginal equivalences of the General Optimum are nevertheless interesting conditions, and it is worth considering how unrealistic the assumption of perfect divisibility is in fact likely to be. It is important to distinguish between consumers' goods (which enter into one or more individual utility functions) and capital goods (which do not). Let us consider the latter first.

† Note that this is true only when there are no external effects in consumption—i.e. when social and private rates of indifference coincide. When they do not coincide, the social rates can, as we saw in Chapter III, only be defined with reference to a particular W. The marginal equivalences of the General Optimum are then a complete set of necessary conditions for reaching that point on the welfare frontier in which the particular W employed in defining social rates of indifference attains a constrained maximum. But when external effects are not present in consumption the statement in the text holds—the marginal equivalences of the General Optimum have no necessary connection with any particular W.

CAPITAL GOODS

It is improbable that indivisibility is important in connection with capital goods *about to be produced*. One can, generally speaking, plan to build a ship, a machine or a factory of *any* size within wide limits. One does not have to think in terms of indivisible lumps or jumps. That it may not be *profitable* to build machines of non-standard size is another matter altogether. From a purely technical point of view there may be no reason why size should not vary continuously.†

But significant indivisibilities are almost certain to occur when we turn to *produced means of production*. Even if we could have built a ship slightly larger or smaller, varying its size continuously, once it is built it must be regarded as an indivisible unit. How important this is will depend almost entirely on the length of one of the slices of time we used in our classification of commodities. It will be recalled that physically identical goods belonging to different slices of time were regarded as different commodities. There was the obvious implication that physically identical goods belonging to the same slice of time were members of the same commodity—that they were perfect substitutes for one another. That is to say: everyone was assumed to be indifferent as to the time-pattern of production and purchase *within* a slice. Now if the slice is a day, we may have to choose whether to run the ship between London and France or between London and Holland. It must be put to the one use or the other. But if the slice is a year, the choice may be between making the one trip 182 times and the other 183, or the other way about. The fact that the ship is indivisible is unlikely to be of much consequence.

Let us examine the case where the slice is short enough for an indivisibility to be significant. What will the social production frontier look like? Let us start by assuming that there are only two uses to which our indivisible unit of capital equipment can be put. If we keep it in the first use, we shall get a transformation curve

† Note that we can only call a machine 'twice as big' as one of the standard size if it is a perfect substitute for two of the standard size, four of half the standard size, etc. If this is not the case the machines must be regarded as different (indivisible) commodities.

like T_1T_1 in Fig. 16 between any two consumers' goods, X and Y. If we transfer it to the second, we shall get a second curve, like T_2T_2. There is no need for the two to intersect; and, if they do not, the true production frontier is whichever lies the farther out. But when they do intersect, as they do in the diagram in R, the production frontier is a combination of the two, like T_1RT_2; and the correct allocation of the indivisible unit of capital equipment is to its first or second use according as we want to produce a collection of goods on T_1R or on RT_2.

We cannot say which we want until we are given a welfare function and so are able to draw social indifference curves of the Bergson frontier type which are labelled BB in Fig. 16. If the highest is attained in any point other than R, the analysis of Chapter IV stands. Abstracting from the possibility of excessive external effects, marginal social rates of transformation and indifference are equal (unless we have a boundary maximum). But if (as the diagram indicates) R itself is the optimum point, we do not have the familiar marginal equivalence holding. The production frontier has no slope at R—there is no such thing as *the* marginal rate of transformation. In the simple case we have drawn, there is, however, a definite slope on either side of R;† and it is clear that, if R is to be a true maximum, the slope of the BB curve must lie somewhere in between the two slopes of the production frontier at R.

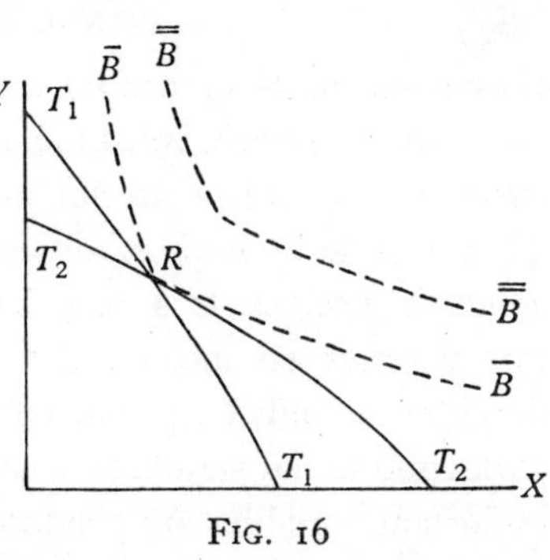

Fig. 16

Thus, if we want to maintain the familiar 'rule' that marginal social rates of indifference and transformation should be equal, we are formally correct in saying that the 'proper' rate of transformation lies between its two values. That is to say: if we find that to increase output it is necessary to use an indivisible unit of capital equipment, so that the marginal cost curve becomes

† Mathematically, both left-hand and right-hand derivatives exist at R.

discontinuous, it is legitimate to regard the 'proper' marginal cost (the one we would, under the usual assumptions,† want equated to price) as lying somewhere between the two extremes.

In more complicated cases, where we have a large number of indivisible units of capital equipment, each capable of a bewildering variety of uses, the production frontier may not be sufficiently well-behaved to have definite slopes on either side of a point like *R*. But rather extreme assumptions have to be made to get results quite as bad as this; ‡ and probably all that will happen in the more complicated cases is that points like *R* (where the frontier has a kink) will be multiplied.

CONSUMERS' GOODS

Indivisible units of capital equipment make the transformation curves between final consumers' goods less smooth than they might otherwise be. They do not normally make them discontinuous. That is done by indivisibilities in the output of final consumers' goods themselves. It is clear that such indivisibilities exist: motor-cars, wireless sets and countless other goods (non-durable as well as durable) can only be produced and purchased in indivisible units.

But too much significance should not be attached to this. The important variables are production and purchase *per slice of time*, and these can clearly vary continuously, at least on the production side. The possibility of smoothing out indivisibilities on the purchase side by distributing expenditure through time depends on the credit-worthiness of the buyer, the availability of hire-purchase agreements, and similar factors. How successful these are likely to be in practice it is difficult to say. In one respect, however, they are not likely to help much in contemporary society. The sale (or negative purchase) of productive services does seem to involve significant indivisibilities—most men have to choose between working an eight-hour day and not working at all. There can be no nice balancing of margins here.

† See Chapter X.

‡ Mathematically, the frontier has to be non-differentiable over a finite range.

Just how important indivisibilities are in fact likely to be in connection with consumers' goods (and services) the reader must decide for himself. But, if he decides that they are important, we can save none of the marginal equivalences. For goods to be correctly allocated among consumers, it is no longer true that the marginal social rate of indifference between any two must be the same for every consumer who consumes them both. On the production side, the analogous rules for the correct allocation of factors no longer hold. The production frontier must be represented by a scatter of discrete points, and the rule that 'proper' marginal cost lies somewhere between its two extremes must also be sacrificed. We can, if we wish, still interpret marginal cost as the slope of a straight line joining two adjacent but discrete points on the frontier; but a little experimentation will convince the reader that there is no reason why the social indifference curve through the optimum point should have a slope somewhere in between the slopes of the straight lines joining it to the 'next best' points on either side.

Indivisibilities in final consumers' goods and the consequent sacrifice of the marginal equivalences have several far-reaching consequences, which are not always appreciated. Here it is sufficient to note one of the more simple and spectacular. Assume that we have an approved distribution of wealth in a community innocent of external effects, and that an indivisible lump of some consumers' good is available. Does it follow that it should go to the man willing to bid the most for it? It does not. The fact that the distribution of wealth is approved merely means that a *marginal* unit of expenditure by any member of the community is judged to make the same contribution to social welfare. It does not mean that an expenditure of £2x by one necessarily makes a greater contribution than an expenditure of £x by another—and this is true whether or not the distribution remains approved after the expenditure has been made. Before it can be said that the expenditure of a finite amount by one man makes a greater contribution to social welfare than the expenditure of a smaller finite amount by another, something to the following effect must be postulated: 'the marginal social significance of money-expenditure (no matter by whom it is made) is constant over the relevant range'. This can only be postulated in terms of a specific W.

All the convenient properties of the price system which enable us to say that (provided the distribution of wealth is approved) goods should go to the highest bidder, or that factors of production should be used where they earn most, break down completely when we have indivisibilities of this sort. We can say nothing without recourse to a definite and well-defined welfare function. It is most important to grasp this point.

CONSUMERS' SURPLUS

The problems raised by finite movements of any sort—and in particular those raised by indivisibilities—are often handled with the aid of consumer's surplus. The reader may wonder why I have avoided it, both in Chapter V (where finite movements were discussed in terms of efficiency loci) and in the present context. There will always be dispute about the appropriateness of various tools of analysis, but I am inclined to regard this particular tool as one which is best eschewed.† The following example may show why.

Consider a simple version of Dupuit's classic problem.‡ An indivisible bridge is to be built across a river. How are we to discover whether or not the investment is worth while? The conventional method of answering the question involves estimating (i) the maximum amount a monopolist could charge consumers if he really could discriminate perfectly between different crossers and different crossings, and (ii) the minimum amount for which he could get the bridge built if he could discriminate perfectly between different units of the various factors of production used in its construction. If it is found that he could make the bridge pay, many would seem to argue that building the bridge is worth while.

† Cf. P. A. Samuelson, *Foundations of Economic Analysis* (Cambridge, Mass., 1947), pp. 195 ff.

‡ Dupuit's 1844 contribution to the *Annales de Ponts et Chaussées* has been reprinted under the heading 'De l'Utilité et de sa Mesure' in *La Riforma Soziale* (Turin, 1932).

In point of fact, however, this method of estimating surpluses is unnecessarily crude. Before the construction of the bridge, one set of prices will prevail; after its construction, another. Recent theoretical work enables us to calculate the gains and losses of consumers' and producers' surplus experienced by each of the various members of the community as a result of this alteration in prices, once its extent is known.† There is no need to restrict ourselves to the surpluses a discriminating monopolist could appropriate. The indirect effects of withdrawing factors of production to build the bridge and the loss of surplus on the goods they used to produce,‡ the lowering of the incomes of ferrymen—these and other matters can and should be taken into account.

Let us suppose that there are but two members of the community affected by the alteration in prices to which the construction of the bridge gives rise. (The price of crossing the bridge is to be thought of as falling to zero, or the amount of the toll, from whatever height would be necessary to eliminate demand entirely.) The money value of the one's gain in surplus is £100; the other's loss of surplus is £90. That is to say: the first man could give up £100 and remain just as well off as he was before the bridge was built; while if the second were paid £90 he too would be just as well off as before. Does it follow that building the bridge is worth while?

Clearly, it does not. There is no reason why welfare should increase in terms of whatever *W* we are employing. But could not the gainer compensate the loser and still remain a gainer? As we saw in Chapter V, it would not make much difference if he could—unless he actually *did*, in which case social welfare would increase on the simple Pareto test: one man being better off, and the other no worse off, than before. In the absence of compensation actually

† J. R. Hicks, 'The Generalized Theory of Consumer's Surplus', *Review of Economic Studies*, vol. XIII (2) (1945–6), pp. 68–74. For simplicity of exposition I have ignored the fact that there are at least four different kinds of surplus.

‡ One occasionally meets in the literature a suggestion to the effect that there is no need to worry about this loss of surplus if the factors are perfectly divisible and withdrawn *from the margins* of their alternative employments. Perhaps it is worth pointing out that finite quantities of factors (such as are needed to build a bridge) can never be drawn from a finite number of margins. A finite sum of infinitesimal quantities is still an infinitesimal.

being paid, the fact that it could be merely means that the efficiency locus of the second situation passes outside the point representing the first. We cannot say more until we have a definite *W*—although, if we were told that the second locus lay wholly outside the first *locus*, we could say that the bridge was 'potentially desirable'.

But do the figures of a £100 gain and a £90 loss in fact mean that compensation could be paid? That is: can we in fact use the techniques of surplus analysis to give us information about local movements in efficiency loci? The answer is that we cannot—at least, not without very complicated adjustments. The sums of £100 and £90 are calculated on the basis of a definite alteration in prices. If compensation were to be paid prices would alter still further—the extent of the alteration depending on the amount of compensation paid. A positive aggregate surplus of £10 at pre-compensation prices can easily translate itself into a negative one if recomputed on the basis of the prices which would rule if compensation were paid, in whole or in part.

Doubtless the surplus computations can be adjusted to meet this difficulty, but they seem to become very unwieldy. The crux of the matter is that trying to measure changes in ordinal well-being in terms of money (or in terms of any other commodity) does not help as the welfare significance of a unit of money depends on prices, and therefore on how much money other people have to spend.† It is simpler to tackle the problems raised by finite movements of any sort (and in particular by indivisibilities) quite directly, as we did in Chapter V. Any point on one of the diagrams of Chapter V represents a definite amount of ordinal utility for each of the members of the community. A movement to another point registers a change in these amounts. That is all we need know. Nothing is gained in trying to obtain money measures of the changes—which is what the surplus enthusiasts try to do.

It is sometimes claimed for surplus analysis that it can be used

† It will be noted that this criticism holds whether or not the welfare significance of money to an individual man is independent of the amount he already has—i.e. whether or not the 'marginal utility of money' is constant to the man concerned.

to show why production may be socially advantageous even if receipts do not cover costs. That may well be true, but the same conclusion can be reached by more direct methods. Indeed, I suspect that the whole habit of measuring finite gains and losses in monetary terms—which is a habit the use of consumer's surplus encourages—is apt to be definitely misleading. It leads naturally to unthinking acceptance of statements like 'it is better to invest in *A* rather than *B* because, taking the possibilities of discrimination into account, it could be more profitable'. Subject to all the usual qualifications about external effects and the distribution of income, it is of course perfectly valid to say that an infinitesimal (or marginal) increment of investment is best applied where the return is highest. But it is quite without foundation if said of a finite or indivisible increment. To provide it with some foundation we must postulate that the marginal social significance of money expenditure (no matter by whom expended) is constant over the relevant range. This can only be done in terms of a well-defined *W*.

We are back where we started. The use of consumer's surplus analysis does not help us to avoid the one really fundamental difficulty. Where questions involving finite movements or indivisibilities are involved, the distribution of wealth is bound to be affected. Thus, unless everybody's welfare is affected in the same way (or unless an efficiency locus *shifts* either inwards or outwards, so that we can talk of 'potential benefit'), we cannot avoid making interpersonal comparisons. Doubtless many would argue that if the indivisibility is 'small' the distribution will not be affected 'much', so that a wide variety of *W*'s will tell the same story about the direction in which social welfare moves. That may well be true, but it does not alter the fact that we require much more specific value judgements (i.e. a rather more closely defined *W*) as soon as we want to take indivisibilities into account.

CHAPTER VIII

UNCERTAINTY

This chapter poses very briefly a number of problems, none of which it attempts to solve. They fall naturally into two classes. The one is concerned with the formation of a social attitude to uncertainty; the other with the way in which uncertainty increases the number and range of the types of variable which we must allow to have a direct influence on welfare. But first a comment on the sense in which the word is used.†

Uncertainty is not to be thought of as a quantitative thing like the chance or numerical probability of a coin showing heads when tossed a large number of times. It refers to something qualitative. It is a description of a degree of knowledge, or lack of knowledge. It arises whenever one has incomplete information on which to act. The problem of acting 'rationally' in the face of uncertainty is not the problem of maximizing the actuarial value of anticipated gains, or minimizing the actuarial value of anticipated losses—if either of these is in any sense 'rational'; ‡ it is the problem of making the best use of incomplete information.

† Cf. F. H. Knight, *Risk, Uncertainty and Profit* (reissued, London, 1933).

‡ Marshall, and a succession of writers dating back to Daniel Bernoulli, have suggested that, when confronted with choices involving *risk* (not uncertainty), men would try to maximize the mathematical expectation or actuarial value of the (cardinal) *utilities* of the gains—not of the gains themselves, measured in monetary terms. Recently the theory has been axiomatized by Professors von Neumann and Morgenstern, who in effect define utility as the quantity whose mathematical expectation is maximized. As I have indicated in Chapter III, I believe their treatment to be unsatisfactory. But more recently still it has been suggested by Professor Marschak, not that men *will* maximize the mathematical expectation of utility, but that they *should* do so. He terms such behaviour 'rational'—and uses the word in a normative sense. I can see no justification whatever for such a procedure. Assuming that some meaning other than 'the quantity whose mathematical expectation is maximized' (if indeed such a quantity exists) can be given to cardinal utility, why should a man be termed 'irrational' if he cares to pay heed to the skewness of the distribution of expected utilities? Of course, 'irrationality' can be *defined* in this way. But then there is no excuse for attaching to it a *normative* connotation.

Cf. A. Marshall, *Principles of Economics* (8th ed., 1920), pp. 135, 842–3. For Bernoulli's views, see I. Todhunter, *A History of the Mathematical Theory of Probability* (Cambridge and London, 1865), Chap. XI. Further references are contained in M. Friedman and L. J. Savage, 'The Utility Analysis of Choices

Whether or not we should apply the term 'uncertainty' to the outcome of a *single* toss of a coin involves questions of great subtlety which are largely irrelevant in the present context.† It is sufficient to note that if we choose to discuss the matter under the heading of 'risk' or 'probability', most of what is said in the next two sections applies to these concepts just as much as to 'uncertainty'.‡

SOCIAL ATTITUDE TO UNCERTAINTY

In the preceding chapters we avoided many questions by assuming that the observing economist knew all about tastes and techniques this side of the horizon. In the real world no one possesses such knowledge. Men may agree that marginal social rates of transformation and indifference should be equated, but disagree fundamentally on what these rates are. Their disagreement may be based on differences in the way they themselves regard the probable course of future events, or on differences in the way they assess the reliability of the estimates of others. The common argument for *laissez faire*, that a man whose personal finances are tied up with the future of a concern is likely to make more reliable estimates than a salaried bureaucrat, and the common reply that

Involving Risk', *Journal of Political Economy*, vol. LIV (1948), pp. 279–304. Cf. also J. von Neumann and O. Morgenstern, *Theory of Games and Economic Behavior* (Princeton, 1944), especially appendix to 1947 edition; Jacob Marschak, 'Rational Behavior, Uncertain Prospects, and Measurable Utility', *Econometrica*, vol. XVIII (2) (1950), pp. 111–41.

† On the general problems raised in trying to assess the 'probability' of a unique event, see G. L. S. Shackle, *Expectation in Economics* (Cambridge, 1949); also Ralph Turvey, J. de V. Graaff and W. J. Baumol, and G. L. S. Shackle, 'Three Notes on *Expectation in Economics*', *Economica*, vol. XVI (1949), pp. 336–46.

‡ The reader familiar with Professor Sir Harold Jeffreys's *Theory of Probability* (London, 1939) may find the following comment helpful. We simply do not know whether a coin will show heads or tails when tossed once. The conventional assignation of equal 'prior probabilities' to each of the two possible outcomes is a precise way of admitting our ignorance. The problems raised by uncertainty are essentially those of assigning 'prior probabilities' in the very much more complicated case where we have a suspicion that the coin is biased, and in the more realistic cases (not involving coins at all) where we have—or think we have—some slight knowledge of the situation. The crux of the argument of the next section of this chapter is that the assignation of 'prior probabilities' is essentially arbitrary and will be done differently by different men, who are therefore unlikely to agree on the proper course of action to take in a given situation.

the bureaucrat is likely to have more information at his disposal, provides an obvious example.

When we admit considerations of this nature we must recognize that interpersonal comparisons, not of well-being, but of reliability of judgement, are required at a very early stage in welfare analysis. If there is no agreed basis on which to make them, we cannot progress very far. Moreover, even if there is an agreed basis, we have a further difficulty to meet.

Let us suppose that, after weighing the estimates of the experts, all men are agreed that the outcome of a particular event will be either *A* or *B*. There is, we suppose, no sense in which one is more likely than the other: there is simple ignorance as to which will occur. It is clear that men may disagree on the proper or 'rational' course of action to take. If it is a matter on which each can go his own way, this is of no consequence. But if it is a matter on which collective action must be taken, definite value judgements are required as to what constitutes the 'rational' course.† Some men will be willing to gamble on the most favourable outcome materializing; others will want to prepare for the worst. A third group will prefer to make their plans as flexible as possible, so that neither contingency will catch them wholly unprepared. How is a balance to be struck without interpersonal comparisons of some sort? ‡

Note that this difficulty is quite independent of the one which would arise if all men were not agreed that the outcome would be either *A* or *B*, or if some believed one to be more probable than the other. Further interpersonal comparisons are required to deal with that situation, if a social attitude is to be formed. There are, in fact, three distinct stages at which interpersonal comparisons

† I put 'rational' in inverted commas because there is, of course, no reason why anyone should want to select, or regard as proper, that which someone else chooses to term 'rational'—or, indeed, what he himself terms 'rational'.

‡ I avoid the question of just what sort of interpersonal comparisons are required. Many economists would be prepared to say that they are ordinary interpersonal comparisons of the 'utility' or 'disutility' the different men would derive from the 'risk-bearing' (some would say 'uncertainty-bearing') involved. It is, however, not easy to define these terms satisfactorily, and it seems unnecessary to go into the matter.

are required—or three separate reasons why men may fail to agree on the desirability of a particular event:

(i) They may evaluate differently the contribution any one man's well-being makes to social well-being—that is, they may have different *W*'s.

(ii) Even if they have identical *W*'s, they may disagree on the probable consequences of the event, or on the order of likelihood of those consequences—either because their own estimates of the situation differ or because they evaluate differently the reliability of the estimates of others.

(iii) Even if they agree on the probable consequences and their ordering, they may disagree on the 'proper' way to allow for the uncertainty involved—on whether to prepare for the worst or gamble on the best.

Without a substantial measure of agreement on these three matters there is bound to be dispute on the desirability of particular events; and the economist is quite unable to say what their effects on welfare are likely to be.

A final comment on (iii) may not be out of place. Very often it seems to be implied that the reduction of uncertainty—the provision of more complete information about the present or the future—is bound to increase welfare. One can easily disagree with such a view without going to the opposite extreme and proclaiming that 'ignorance is bliss'. Much of the excitement of life would vanish if we knew too much of the future.† It would be a rather curious use of words if we were to find ourselves saying that welfare has increased, when all we mean is that life has become exceedingly dull. There is probably an optimum amount of uncertainty for any system.

NEW TYPES OF VARIABLE

Hitherto we have been considering a man's welfare over the whole period of his life (or at least over that part of it lying this side of the horizon), and we have regarded it as a function of the goods

† The completely stultifying effect of really perfect foresight is well known. Cf. O. Morgenstern, 'Vollkommene Voraussicht und wirtschaftliches Gleichgewicht', *Zeitschrift für Nationalökonomie*, vol. VI (1935).

and services he would actually consume and render during the various slices of time within that period. But now we must start taking account of the fact that these actual quantities are not known to anyone but the hypothetical observing economist. Looking back over his life, any man will admit that his well-being has depended not only on the actual quantities of goods and services consumed and rendered, but also on his anticipations, at any time, of what he believed he would consume and render in the future—and not on his anticipations alone, but also on the confidence with which they were held.

Anticipations and the confidence with which they are held (which is the inverse of the uncertainty involved in the situation) enter quite directly into the determination of welfare. Our hopes and fears for the future should enter our utility functions quite explicitly—for they certainly affect our choices.† But as soon as we let them we have to revise the majority of our conclusions, which have all been based on a very strict adherence to the rule that welfare depends only on actual quantities; and we have to change our attitude on a number of points. Let us take an example.

Social institutions have hitherto only been considered in so far as they affected the variables we allowed to play a direct part in the determination of welfare—the flow of goods and services. But if they shape our attitude to the future—if monopoly is favoured because it holds out the prospect of a quiet life—this procedure is clearly illegitimate. Social institutions may become ends in themselves, and may not just be means to the attainment of more outputs and fewer inputs, as we have hitherto regarded them. The market-mechanism itself provides a good example. A man may feel that its decisions are in some sense impersonal and unbiased, and he may prefer to have prices determined and income distributed by it rather than by some bureaucrat, at whose hands he may fear victimization—even if the bureaucrat saw to the satisfaction

† I phrase it in this way to maintain the crude behaviourist concept of welfare with which we set out. But if we are prepared to accept for a moment something a little more hedonistic, it is surely clear that we *enjoy by anticipation*—and just as much as in the act—or by recollection. Cf. G. L. S. Shackle, *Expectation in Economics* (Cambridge, 1949), esp. Chap. II.

of the marginal equivalences of the General Optimum much better than the market.

In a similar way *prices* must be allowed to play a direct part in influencing welfare, not just because they may be used as an index of quality or snob-appeal, but because they affect anticipations of future income. As soon as we include them in utility functions, we find that we can derive none of the familiar marginal equivalences as necessary conditions for maximum welfare.

There is not really much point in giving further examples. The crux of the matter is that the majority of the conventional results of welfare economics depend very intimately on the way in which we circumscribe the list of variables in the individual utility functions. In Chapter I we recognized that there were variables other than those conventionally considered (the 'economic' ones), but we decided to assume for a while that they were exogenous (i.e. that, although they influenced the economic ones, they were uninfluenced by them—like the weather). But it is clear that market prices are in no sense exogenous. Nor are market forms (like the monopoly which gives the quiet life). Their admission disrupts the entire fabric of conventional welfare theory.

Apart from pointing this out, and emphasizing it, there is little we can say. We have come to a stage at which we are really ready to start evaluating the significance of all that has gone before. But before turning to evaluation, it is instructive to apply what results we have derived to a few special problems. This is done in the three chapters that follow.

CHAPTER IX

FOREIGN TRADE

When a community establishes trading relations with foreigners, it is usually able to transform goods of one kind into goods of another kind more readily than before. The process of transformation need no longer be confined to domestic factories. It can be carried out by trade abroad. Unless the terms on which, before trade starts, one good can be exchanged for another in the foreign market are exactly the same as the rate at which the one can be transformed into the other at home, access to the foreign market is clearly equivalent to an outward shift of the social production frontier.†

So far we have done no more than state the classical doctrine of comparative costs in a refined form; but we can go a stage further. Unless there are excessive external effects in consumption in the domestic economy, the outward shift of the production frontier will (except in a limiting case) result in an outward shift of the welfare frontier. In this sense, therefore, *some* trade is always at least potentially beneficial.‡ As Ricardo put it, it will 'increase the mass of commodities, and therefore the sum of enjoyments'.§ But what is the *optimum amount* of trade? Is it the amount realized under free trade? The answer is that it is not—except under quite exceptional circumstances. The argument involves the classical discussion of Tariffs and the Terms of Trade,

† For a diagrammatic treatment, see R. E. Baldwin, 'Equilibrium in International Trade: A Diagrammatic Analysis', *Quarterly Journal of Economics*, vol. LXII (1948), pp. 748–62. It should be emphasized that both the statement in the text and Baldwin's treatment are valid only if we assume the absence of *international* external effects in *production*. These are discussed below.

‡ Cf. P. A. Samuelson, 'The Gains from International Trade', *Canadian Journal of Economics and Political Science*, vol. V (1939), pp. 195–205. Both Samuelson's treatment and the statement in the text about an outward shift of the welfare frontier assume the absence of *international* external effects in *consumption*. These are discussed below.

§ *Works and Correspondence of David Ricardo*, ed. P. Sraffa, vol. I (Cambridge, 1951), pp. 128–9.

which is reserved for the next section. Let us look at the matter in a slightly different way first.†

If we regard the whole world as the group whose welfare we want to maximize, and if we have conditions favourable for the achievement of the General Optimum by perfect competition, free trade will be optimal in the sense that it leads to the world's welfare frontier. But we may not approve of the distribution of welfare among the people (or peoples) of the world to which it leads—we may not approve of the particular point on the frontier at which it lands us. And, if we are interested in maximizing the welfare of a particular nation, rather than of the whole world, we are certain to prefer a movement along the (multidimensional) frontier in a direction which favours the nationals with whom we are concerned. Such a movement can in theory be brought about by lump-sum redistributions of wealth. But it is beyond the power of most nations to secure these in their favour, except after victorious wars. They can, however, 'tax the foreigner' by means of measures which are not lump-sum—by taxing imports and exports. In doing so they destroy the world-wide attainment of the General Optimum, and disrupt the allocative efficiency of the world economy; but they achieve a movement *off and within* the world's welfare frontier in a direction favourable to themselves.

TARIFFS AND THE TERMS OF TRADE

The process whereby any one country can achieve a favourable movement within the world's welfare frontier by taxing imports and exports is generally called 'turning the terms of trade in its favour'. To a certain extent this is unfortunate, as 'the terms of trade' (like an 'industry' and several other concepts) is much more useful a tool in positive economics than in welfare theory;‡ but it does give a vivid idea of a country curtailing both imports and

† Cf. P. A. Samuelson, 'Welfare Economics and International Trade', *American Economic Review*, vol. XXVIII (1938), pp. 261–6.

‡ Except in a two-commodity world, the 'terms of trade' cannot be unambiguously defined unless we have a definite welfare function—just as, except in a two-commodity world (i.e. one in which there is a numéraire and one other good), we can only define the true cost-of-living index when we know the consumer's utility function.

exports, forcing the prices of the former down and those of the latter up on the world market, and benefiting both as a monopsonist and a monopolist.

In this form the argument dates back to John Stuart Mill †—if not Torrens and Ricardo;‡ but its refined formulation is essentially due to Bickerdike § and Edgeworth, || writing at the turn of the century. In recent years it has been revived and restated by a number of contemporary economists, ¶ and it is now widely known.

It is, however, equally instructive to think of the process as one whereby the country attains its own (as distinct from the world's) welfare frontier. To do so it must secure the satisfaction of a familiar set of marginal equivalences, one of which is the following: for any two traded goods which are also produced at home, *the marginal social rate of transformation through foreign trade must be equal to the marginal social rate of transformation in domestic factories.*†† That is to say: the rate at which more X must be exported to get more Y (if it is an import; or to retain more of it, if it is another export) must be equal to the rate at which X must be sacrificed (if it is an output; or expended, if it is an input) to

† J. S. Mill, *Essays on Some Unsettled Questions of Political Economy* (London, 1844), pp. 24–36 of L.S.E. reprint 1948.

‡ Cf. J. Viner, *Studies in the Theory of International Trade* (New York, 1937), pp. 298–9 and 320.

§ C. F. Bickerdike, 'The Theory of Incipient Taxes', *Economic Journal*, vol. XVI (1906), pp. 529 ff.; and his review of Pigou's *Protective and Preferential Import Duties* (*Economic Journal*, vol. XVII (1907), pp. 98 ff.).

|| F. Y. Edgeworth, *Papers Relating to Political Economy*, vol. II (1925), pp. 340 ff. (Reprinted from the 1908 *Economic Journal*.) Edgeworth was remarkably reluctant to admit that free trade was not really best—cf. pp. 365–6, where he hints that the whole investigation should be labelled POISON.

¶ A. P. Lerner, 'The Diagrammatical Representation of Demand Conditions in International Trade', *Economica*, New Series, vol. I (1934), p. 333, *idem*, *The Economics of Control* (New York, 1944), pp. 382–5. N. Kaldor, 'A Note on Tariffs and the Terms of Trade', *Economica*, New Series, vol. VII (1940). T. de Scitovsky, 'A Reconsideration of the Theory of Tariffs', *Review of Economic Studies*, vol. IX (2) (1941–2), pp. 89–110. Stephen Enke, 'The Monopsony Case for Tariffs', *Quarterly Journal of Economics*, vol. LVIII (1944), pp. 229–45. Joan Robinson, 'The Pure Theory of International Trade', *Review of Economic Studies*, vol. XIV (2) (1946–7), pp. 107–8. R. F. Kahn, 'Tariffs and the Terms of Trade', *Review of Economic Studies*, vol. XV (1) (1947–8), pp. 14–19. I. M. D. Little, 'Welfare and Tariffs', *Review of Economic Studies*, vol. XVI (2) (1948–9), pp. 65–70. J. de V. Graaff, 'On Optimum Tariff Structures', *Review of Economic Studies*, vol. XVII (2) (1949–50), pp. 47–59.

†† Cf. appendix to this chapter, equation (9).

get more Y produced at home. If it is not, we can clearly get (or retain) more of both goods by reshuffling.

Naturally, as with all the other marginal conditions we have encountered, we have an *inequality* to be satisfied if one of the goods is not traded, or is not produced at home; and naturally, too, the rule is valid only on certain assumptions. With the first two the reader will be familiar—they formed the basis of the analogous rules for closed economies we set out in an earlier chapter—the horizon and terminal capital (including terminal foreign assets or debt) † must be given, and the production functions must be independent of the distribution of wealth. Thirdly, the domestic and foreign production functions must not be interrelated—there must be no *international* external effects in production. If there are (as there may be when a country draws a portion of its labour force from abroad, or will be when a polluted river harms two countries) the rule becomes rather more complicated.‡

On these three assumptions, the satisfaction of the rule is necessary for the attainment of the open-economy's production frontier. It ensures that we cannot get more of any one output or import without sacrificing others, or expending more inputs or exports. As before, however, it is only when excessive external effects in domestic consumption are ruled out that we necessarily want to attain the production frontier. This is the fourth assumption. The fifth is that domestic welfare is unaffected by the consumption of foreigners—that there are no *international* external effects in consumption in this direction. If there are (as when domestic welfare grows with the armaments of allies and diminishes with those of enemies, or when the domestic conscience is plagued by the thought of famine abroad), domestic welfare may be maximized somewhere *within* the production frontier. Thus we may refuse to export radioactive minerals for fear that they will be used

† In Chapter VI we argued that decisions affecting terminal capital are likely to be among the most important a community has to make. The same applies to terminal foreign debt. It determines the whole attitude to balance-of-payments policy.

‡ Cf. appendix, equations (6)–(8).

against us by our enemies, although by exporting them we may be able to get more of every commodity.

Finally, it is to be emphasized that the rule is but *one of several* necessary for the attainment of the General Optimum in an open economy. Another important one, true on the same five assumptions, is that *marginal social rates of indifference and transformation* (*both at home and through trade*) *must be equal* for any two goods which are consumed and produced domestically and traded internationally. All the marginal equivalences must be satisfied *simultaneously* if the welfare frontier is to be attained. If some are not satisfied, the satisfaction of others may lead away from the frontier. Thus, in an environment in which perfect competition would be optimal, the protection afforded by a tax on imports might give birth to monopoly, and thus disrupt the allocative efficiency of the economy by destroying the equality of rates of transformation and indifference. In the language of Chapter V, the tax may twist, or shift inwards, the domestic efficiency locus—even if it does represent an outward shift of the domestic welfare frontier, as compared with the free-trade situation.†

Keeping these qualifications in mind, let us return to the rule itself and see what it means. If the domestic country can take world prices as fixed (either because it is very small in relation to the world, or because they really are fixed) the marginal social rate of transformation through foreign trade of one good into another is equal to the ratio of their prices on the world market. If the price of X is \$2 and the price of Y \$1, two units of Y can be traded for one unit of X. Now, if (as we shall assume) conditions in the domestic economy are favourable for the free working of the price mechanism (corrected, perhaps, by taxes of the sort we have encountered in earlier chapters), the marginal social rate of

† This distinction is closely akin to the classical one between revenue duties and protecting duties. The burden of the former can be thrown on to the foreigner, through the movement of the terms of trade; whereas the latter, which disrupt the allocative efficiency of the economy, 'are purely mischievous', to use Mill's phrase. (Cf. J. S. Mill, *Essays on . . . Political Economy* (L.S.E. reprint), pp. 26–8, and *Principles* (ed. W. J. Ashby, London, 1909), Book v, Chapter iv, 6.) The distinction should not be pressed too far, however, as any actual duty cannot but be a compound of the two: it will affect the welfare frontier and the efficiency locus in different degrees.

transformation in domestic factories will be equal to the ratio of their domestic prices. But domestic and foreign price ratios are equal under universal free trade; so free trade will satisfy the rule under these conditions.

It is, however, only when the domestic country can take world prices as fixed that free trade necessarily satisfies the rule—although it may do so 'by accident' in circumstances analysed in the next section. When world prices vary, the sale of an extra unit of X by the domestic country will yield a *marginal social revenue* different from its price. 'Normally', we should expect marginal revenue to be less than price, but it is quite possible (when we take into account the effect of the extra X on the prices of *other* goods, imports as well as exports, now and in the future) for it to exceed it. Similarly, the *marginal social cost* of importing more Y will 'normally' exceed its price, but may lie below it.

Now the marginal social rate of transformation through foreign trade of an export into an import is just the ratio of marginal social revenue to marginal social cost. For two exports, or two imports, it is the ratio of marginal revenues, or marginal costs. In every case these must be equated to domestic price ratios (and hence to domestic rates of transformation) if the General Optimum is to be attained by the domestic country. Clearly, the equation can be secured by imposing taxes on both imports and exports to cover the divergence of their prices from marginal social costs and revenues—or, if foreign trade is engaged in by large private concerns, the divergence of their marginal private costs and revenues from the social ones. Such taxes should discriminate not only between different imports and exports, but between those coming from and going to different foreign markets. Clearly, too, taxes are but one method of securing the equation. Multiple exchange rates will do equally well.

The taxes are at least potentially beneficial in the sense that they lead the domestic country to its welfare frontier (or shift it outwards, as compared with the free trade situation). Once they have been imposed, wealth can be so redistributed as to make every member of the domestic community better off than under free trade.†

FORMULÆ FOR OPTIMUM TAXES

Professor Kahn has recently revived Bickerdike's argument that the 'small' protective tariff, which many economists have favoured for its effect on the terms of trade, may in fact be quite a 'large' one.‡ To assess this claim we must derive a formula for the optimum tariff. We proceed on the following assumptions:§

(i) Horizon, terminal capital and terminal foreign debt are given.

(ii) *International* external effects exist in neither production nor consumption.

(iii) Domestic external effects in consumption are not excessive.

† Professor Scitovsky's admirable analysis of the problem ('A Reconsideration of the Theory of Tariffs', *Review of Economic Studies*, vol. IX (2) (1941–2), pp. 89–110, reprinted as Chapter XVI of *Readings in the Theory of International Trade* (Philadelphia, 1949)) does not make this quite clear, since he bases his welfare judgements on but two of the infinity of possible distributions of wealth —viz. that obtaining in the free trade situation, and that obtaining once the tariff has been imposed (cf. our discussion of the 'Scitovsky test' in Chapter V). Arguments based on an outward shift of the welfare frontier, on the other hand, are valid for all distributions of wealth.

The reader familiar with Scitovsky's analysis will recall that he employs (in a two-commodity world) Marshallian offer curves superimposed on a set of community indifference loci, and that he is careful to distinguish cases where the community indifference loci intersect between the points representing free trade and the optimum degree of protection from cases where they do not intersect. In the former we can, on his welfare criteria, make no statement about the desirability of the tariff; in the latter we can say that it is desirable. What our analysis (which runs along rather different lines) has shown is, in effect, that the community indifference loci can *never* intersect in the relevant range, unless the allocative efficiency of the economy is impaired—i.e. unless the efficiency locus is shifted inwards, or twisted. I say 'in effect' because it is rather difficult to translate our results into Scitovsky's language—he considers an exchange-economy rather than one in which production is allowed to take place. Moreover, although our definition of the Scitovsky frontier in Chapter III is based on his definition of a community indifference locus, it is not quite clear how firmly he abides by the rule that the collection of goods must be optimally distributed. If the community indifference loci are interpreted as analogues of efficiency loci (rather than welfare frontiers), it is quite possible for them to intersect in the way he suggests.

‡ R. F. Kahn, 'Tariffs and the Terms of Trade', *Review of Economic Studies*, vol. XV (1) (1947–8), pp. 14–19. Bickerdike, it will be recalled, argued that 'rather strong assumptions have to be made . . . if the rate of tax affording maximum advantage is to come below 10 per cent' (review of Pigou's *Protective and Preferential Import Duties*, in *Economic Journal*, vol. XVII (1907), p. 101).

§ The reader who wishes to skip the mathematical portions of this section is advised to familiarize himself with these assumptions and then to turn to the geometrical analysis of the two-good case given in the following section.

(iv) *Domestic price ratios reflect domestic marginal social rates of transformation and indifference.*†

(v) *Retaliation is ruled out.*

(vi) Exchange rates are fixed, and assumed to be uniform (i.e. non-multiple), but prices and wages are flexible.

Let us adopt the following notation:

Π_i = domestic price of ith good.‡

p_i = foreign price of ith good.

z_i = net import of ith good into the domestic country. (When z_i is negative it means that the ith good is exported.)

K = terminal foreign debt—i.e. the net provision to be made for foreign lending this side of the horizon. (We shall assume K to be independent of prices; this affects the details, but not the substance of the argument.)

$F = \Sigma p_i z_i + K = 0$. (This means that, correct provision being made for foreign lending, trade must balance. That is, it tells us the maximum amount we can get of any import, given the amounts of our exports and remaining imports, or the minimum amount we must give of any export, given the amounts of our imports and remaining exports. We shall therefore call F the *foreign trade transformation function.*)§

a_i = algebraic difference between marginal social cost (or revenue) and price of the ith good. (Thus $p_i + a_i$ is the marginal social cost of importing the ith good, or the marginal social revenue derived from its sale, if it is an export.)

Now we know that the marginal social rate of transformation

† If there are external effects (in either production or consumption) which call for corrective taxes, these taxes are superimposed on the domestic prices. The basic prices (which no one may pay but on the basis of which all corrective taxes will be calculated) are the ones which reflect the social rates of transformation and indifference.

‡ Physically identical things relating to different slices of time are still different goods.

§ When the foreign market is a competitive one, the equation $F=0$ defines the multidimensional analogue of the foreign country's Marshallian offer curve. But when monopoly, all-or-none offers, etc., characterize the foreign market, F will be something different.

through foreign trade is equal to the ratio of marginal social costs (or revenues). That is to say

$$\frac{\partial F/\partial z_i}{\partial F/\partial z_j}=\frac{p_i+\sum\limits_s \frac{\partial p_s}{\partial z_i}z_s}{p_j+\sum\limits_s \frac{\partial p_s}{\partial z_j}z_s}=\frac{p_i+a_i}{p_j+a_j}. \tag{1}$$

This equation is all we require. We want to secure that rates of transformation through trade equal domestic price-ratios (since, by assumption (iv), these are equal to domestic rates of transformation and indifference), so we must have

$$\frac{p_i+a_i}{p_j+a_j}=\frac{\Pi_i}{\Pi_j}. \tag{2}$$

This is a mathematical statement of the 'rule'.

In the exceptional case where a_i/a_j is fortuitously proportional to p_i/p_j, the equation (2) holds whenever domestic prices are proportional to foreign prices—as they always are under free trade, whatever the exchange rate. In this exceptional case, therefore, free trade establishes the General Optimum from the domestic country's point of view; but it is likely to be a very exceptional case, since the a's will 'normally' be negative for exports (because marginal revenue falls short of price) and positive for imports (because marginal cost exceeds price).

A special version of the exceptional case is where the a's are zero—i.e. where prices do not diverge from marginal costs or revenues. This may be because the a's (as defined by the summations in (1)) just happen to 'add up' to zero; or because they are *identically* zero, in which event the domestic country can take world prices as fixed. It then has no monopolistic or monopsonistic powers to exploit.

In the more general case it will be necessary to adjust domestic prices (since foreign prices are not within our control) to secure the satisfaction of the rule. The simplest method of adjustment is an *ad valorem* tax. If the marginal private costs and revenues of those engaged in international trade do not diverge from prices (i.e. if they are atomistic traders), we must tax to cover the full divergence of social costs and revenues from prices. Equation (2) tells us that domestic prices must *exceed* foreign prices by a_i. Thus we must *tax* imports, and *subsidize* exports, at the *ad valorem* rate a_i/p_i, calculated on the foreign price. The result is to secure

$$\frac{\Pi_i}{\Pi_j} = \frac{p_i(1 + a_i/p_i)}{p_j(1 + a_j/p_j)}, \tag{3}$$

which is just what we require.

At first sight it may seem strange that exports have to be subsidized at the rate a_i/p_i, but it is not. Marginal revenue 'normally' falls short of price, so a_i is 'normally' negative for exports. The subsidy is thus in fact 'normally' a tax.

It is worth noting that *ad valorem* taxes are not the only means of achieving the satisfaction of the rule. Multiple exchange rates can be just as effective. And if bulk-purchase agreements are favoured, we have simply to interpret the 'price' as the 'average cost' (or revenue). The rule defined by equation (2) is still valid; but the government must secure its satisfaction quite directly, by varying the size and terms of the agreement.†

Let us now see what happens to our expression for the optimum taxes if we make the assumption that all 'cross-elasticities' of demand and supply vanish identically on the world market—i.e. that when we import or export more of any good, *its* price is the only one affected.‡ First note, however, that this is a very unrealistic assumption to make. Even if all goods were independent in production (i.e. if all factors of production were completely specific), they would still compete for the consumer's purse—unless the demand for each of them had unit elasticity. Whenever there is some degree of substitutability in production, and demand schedules are not thus circumscribed, an appreciable error may be involved in assuming that all 'cross-elasticities' vanish identically. Even when they are unimportant individually, their combined

† The foreign trade transformation function will change as the form of market organization changes (e.g. from trading at uniform prices to all-or-none offers). The a_i will therefore have different values under bulk-purchase agreements, but the equation (2) must still hold.

‡ Mathematically, p_i is a function of z_i only. This has the important corollary, used below, that $\partial p_i/\partial z_i$ and $\partial z_i/\partial p_i$ are reciprocals.

influence may make a considerable difference to marginal social costs and revenues.

Referring to the expression for a_i under the summation sign in equation (1), it will be seen that a_i/p_i reduces to $(\partial p_i/\partial z_i)z_i/p_i$ when we assume that the 'cross-elasticities' vanish identically. That is to say: the optimum tax on an import is equal to the reciprocal of the foreign elasticity of supply, and the optimum tax on an export to the reciprocal of the foreign elasticity of demand. This is Professor Lerner's elegant result, but he does not make clear the somewhat restrictive assumptions on which it is valid.†

The formula which Professor Kahn uses for his estimate of the probable height of an optimum tariff is implicitly based on a similar assumption about the identical vanishing of all 'cross-elasticities' of demand and supply on the foreign market.‡ It refers to a world in which but two goods are traded internationally: one export and one import. Let us denote them by e and m, respectively. We have now but one international price ratio. To make the domestic import-export price ratio diverge from it to the correct extent, we need not tax both imports and exports: a single tax will do the trick (and so would the introduction of one exchange rate for imports, and another for exports). Thus if an *ad valorem* tariff, of rate t, is imposed on imports (the rate being reckoned on the foreign price), we must have, referring to (3):

$$\frac{\Pi_m}{\Pi_e}=\frac{p_m(1+t)}{p_e}=\frac{p_m+a_m}{p_e+a_e}$$

or

$$t=\frac{(a_m/p_m)-(a_e/p_e)}{1+(a_e/p_e)}. \tag{4}$$

When we make the assumption about 'cross-elasticities' vanishing identically we can rewrite (4) as

$$t=\frac{(1/\eta_s)+(1/\eta_d)}{1-(1/\eta_d)} \tag{5}$$

† Lerner, *The Economics of Control* (New York, 1944), pp. 382–5.

‡ Professor Kahn is aware of this when he warns ('Tariffs and the Terms of Trade', *Review of Economic Studies*, vol. XV (1) (1947–8), p. 17) that his 'elasticities' are not true elasticities at all, but what might be called 'elasticities in the Pigou sense'. Cf. A. C. Pigou, *Public Finance* (3rd ed., London, 1947), pp. 199–200.

where η_s is the foreign elasticity of the supply of imports, and η_d the foreign elasticity of demand for exports (taken with a *minus* sign to make it positive).

THE TWO-GOOD CASE

It is sometimes said that formula (5) refers to the 'two-good case', and so it is worth noting that it does not. In equation (4) we employ two prices, and therefore must have, in addition to the export and the import, at least one domestic good (e.g. labour) to play the part of numéraire. In a true two-commodity world we have but one price: that of the one commodity in terms of the other. It is instructive to see what the optimum tariff is under these conditions. That is very quickly done by setting $p_e \equiv 1$ and $p_m = p$ in equation (4). Recalling that, correct provision (K) being made for foreign lending, trade must balance, we obtain without difficulty

$$t = \frac{\dfrac{\partial p}{\partial z_m}\dfrac{z_m}{p} + \dfrac{\partial p}{\partial z_e}\dfrac{z_e + K}{p}}{1 - \dfrac{\partial p}{\partial z_e}\dfrac{z_e + K}{p}} \tag{6}$$

When K is zero, (6) reduces to a formula very similar to (5) in appearance. But it is not quite the same, as $\partial p/\partial z$ and $\partial z/\partial p$ are no longer reciprocals.

It is also instructive to develop the argument geometrically. Let us consider the case where terminal foreign debt is zero, and take exports (which we shall now write X)† as the numéraire. Their price is then unity. The foreign price of imports we shall write p; their domestic price, Π. Imports themselves we shall write M, so that $p = X/M$. As before, the *ad valorem* rate of tariff, calculated on the foreign price, is t. But the domestic price exceeds the foreign price by the height of the tariff, so $p(1 + t) = \Pi$. That is

$$t = \frac{\Pi}{p} - 1 \tag{7}$$

Now we are ready for the geometry.

† The notation is changed because exports were previously negative; here they are positive.

In Fig. 17 OF is the foreign trade transformation curve—which, if competition rules abroad, is no more than the foreign country's Marshallian offer curve. The dotted BB curves are social indifference curves of the Bergson frontier type. The highest is attained by OF in C. Since people do not normally have preferences for imports and exports as such, but only for the commodities imported and exported, the BB curves are drawn up on the understanding that optimal amounts of the two commodities are produced for domestic consumption.

At the optimum point, C, the domestic marginal social rate of

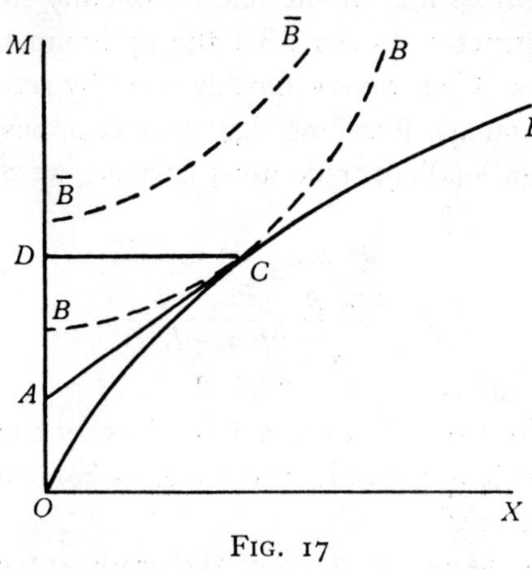

FIG. 17

indifference is DC/DA. This we must have equal to the domestic price ratio, Π. The foreign price ratio, p, is DC/DO. Recalling equation (7), we have

$$t = \frac{DC}{DA} \times \frac{DO}{DC} - 1$$

$$= \frac{DO}{DA} - 1 \quad \text{or} \quad \frac{OA}{DA}. \tag{8}$$

Both forms of (8) are convenient; but the first is perhaps the more so since DO/DA is the elasticity of the foreign offer curve at C.†

† This is easily seen, since

$$\frac{M}{X}\frac{dX}{dM} = \frac{DO}{DC} \cdot \frac{DC}{DA} = \frac{DO}{DA}.$$

From this we can readily translate back into the elasticities of formula (6).

There is one further geometrical property of Fig. 17 that is worth noting. The tariff proceeds are ptM in terms of exports, or ptM/Π in terms of imports. That is

$$\text{tariff proceeds} = \frac{DC}{DO} \cdot \frac{OA}{DA} \cdot DO \cdot \frac{DA}{DC} = OA. \qquad (9)$$

This amount, OA, is returned to consumers in the form of lump-sum payments. When allowed to trade at the domestic price ratio, they then reach C. The distribution of the lump-sum payments is of course made in accordance with the W function defining the social indifference curves, BB.

Note finally that there is no reason why the relative curvature of the social indifference and foreign offer curves should not be such that the optimum, C, coincides with O, where no trade takes place. Then the familiar marginal equality is replaced by an inequality. The point where marginal social rates of indifference and transformation through trade were equal would be a point of minimum, rather than maximum, welfare. That simply emphasizes that, while necessary for a non-boundary maximum, the satisfaction of the rule is by no means sufficient.

THE 'PROBABLE HEIGHT' OF THE TARIFF

Professor Kahn's procedure in estimating the 'probable height' of the optimum tariff from formula (5) is to attribute likely values to the elasticities involved, and see what tariff the formula indicates. This is not legitimate. Whatever the elasticities may be, there can be no escaping the fact that their magnitudes will generally depend upon the height of the tariff. The tariff and the elasticities are not independent—the latter will alter as the tariff varies and moves one to different points on OF in Fig. 17. One relation which must hold between them at the optimum point has been produced, but there are undoubtedly others. Thus, consider the case where the foreign elasticity of demand is unity. This does not mean, as a simple substitution in formula (5) might seem to suggest, that the optimum tariff is infinitely high—for an infinite tariff is not consistent with a demand elasticity of unity. As the tariff grew, one would expect the elasticity to change. Speaking very generally, there is perhaps a presumption that it will increase as the tariff grows; and there is perhaps a further presumption that the foreign supply of imports will become more elastic too. Both these changes would tend to *reduce* the height of the optimum tariff.

It is, therefore, not quite legitimate to make deductions about the probable height of an optimum tariff from so simple a formula as (5). One can never be sure that the values one attributes to the elasticities are, in fact, consistent with the formula the tariff indicates, or with each other.

Once it is recognized that the elasticities depend on the height of the tariff, it is natural to ask if it is possible to establish rather more precisely the nature of the dependence. Into this matter I do not propose to enter. But it is worth remarking that one of the obvious factors influencing the final result is the way in which the tariff affects the *prices* of imports and exports. This in turn depends in part upon the *domestic* elasticities of demand and supply, and so upon the domestic distribution of income.

We have here the resolution of two paradoxes. The first, which has puzzled several writers,† is why the optimum tariff formula should depend upon the foreign elasticities only. The answer is that the formula does not *determine* the tariff in terms of the foreign elasticities; it merely indicates one of several relations which must exist between them at the optimum point. The height of the tariff is not in fact independent of domestic conditions of demand and supply. The second is related to interpersonal comparisons of well-being. How have we been able to determine a unique formula for the optimum tariff without making any? The answer is that, while the formula is unique, the actual tariff it indicates depends very intimately indeed on the domestic distribution of wealth (which is one of the factors determining the consistency of the elements in the formula), and so can only be approved if we approve of the distribution. (In terms of Fig. 17, the optimum

† Cf. R. F. Kahn, 'Tariffs and the Terms of Trade', *Review of Economic Studies*, vol. xv (1) (1947–8), p. 16, bottom.

point depends on the welfare function we use to define the social indifference curves, *BB*.) We have in fact an infinity of optimum tariffs, all determined by the same rule, but each corresponding to a different distribution of wealth. We cannot judge between them without making interpersonal comparisons, and their existence makes it rather hard to attach significance to attempts at discovering the 'probable height' of the tariff, except in terms of a specific and well-defined *W*.

The situation is precisely analogous to that encountered in a closed economy. There we can formulate, on the basis of a long list of assumptions we shall examine in the next chapter, a rule such as 'equate marginal cost to price'. This rule is quite general, but it will not tell us how high prices must be until we know something about the pattern of demand, and therefore the distribution of wealth. Without a welfare function, or some other criterion for judging between different distributions, we cannot say at what level prices and marginal costs are to be equated, and so we can say but little of the 'probable height' of the prices.

It is of course conceivable that the infinity of possible heights of prices and tariffs will occasionally lie within a reasonably narrow range. And in this regard it is worth noting that, far from being in any way 'protectionist', an optimum tariff can conceivably be *negative*.† For instance, when the goods a country imports and those it exports are very close substitutes on the world market, the marginal cost of imports may be *less* than their price (because the additional demand for imports raises the price of exports substantially). In these circumstances a *subsidy* on imports is required. Similarly, a subsidy on exports may be called for when the export of investment goods is likely to lower import prices in the future

† In a true two-commodity world this can only happen when imports are inferior goods in the domestic country—indeed, so markedly inferior that the Giffen Paradox operates. When we have more than two goods such extreme assumptions are not required. (Cf. J. L. Mosak, *General Equilibrium Theory in International Trade* (Bloomington, Ind., 1944), esp. pp. 65–8 and 103–5.) It is interesting to recall that Marshall, in his 'Memorandum on Fiscal Policy', thought that the Giffen Paradox might operate in respect of imports of wheat into England, and pointed out that if it did the effect of a tariff would be to turn the terms of trade against her. (Cf. A. Marshall, *Official Papers* (London, 1926), pp. 382–3.)

to an appreciable extent. If we take into account the possibility of cheap exports precipitating a slump when 'dumped' abroad, or increased imports stimulating world recovery (and thus the demand for our exports), such examples become easy to multiply.

In conclusion it is worth re-emphasizing the assumptions on which the optimum tariff formula is based. If it were ever to be applied, some allowance would have to be made for *retaliation*. It is easiest to think of retaliation as the lowering of the foreign offer curve in Fig. 17 to a new position. If the domestic country readjusts its tariff, the optimum point will still be one where marginal social rates of indifference and transformation through trade are equal, but it will lie on a lower social indifference curve. The same formula between tariff and elasticities must hold, but both tariff and elasticities will have different values.

Some countries may be so favourably situated that, no matter what retaliatory steps its trading partners take, its monopolistic and monopsonistic gains cannot be encroached upon. The conditions under which this is likely to occur are hard to set out theoretically, but it can certainly be envisaged as a possibility. It is more probable, however, that the progressive disruption of the allocative efficiency of the world economy as more and more countries resort to protection will eventually lead to all being worse off than they would have been under free trade—assuming conditions to have been favourable for its existence in the first place ('correct' curvature of production and indifference curves, etc.).

Whatever may happen in this regard, a great deal of guessing and uncertainty is bound to be involved in any attempt to 'make proper allowance' for retaliation. And note that retaliation is to be expected, since it is the rational thing for each country, acting separately, to lower its offer curve to foreigners. There is nothing spiteful about retaliatory behaviour. Each country is led naturally to it in trying to maximize its own welfare.†

† Cf. T. de Scitovsky, 'A Reconsideration of the Theory of Tariffs', *Review of Economic Studies*, vol. IX (2) (1941–2), pp. 100–1 and 109–10; also R. F. Kahn, 'Tariffs and the Terms of Trade', *Review of Economic Studies*, vol. XV (1) (1947–8), pp. 18–19.

The difficult thing for a country to judge is how the speed and extent of foreigners' reactions will be affected by the height of its own tariff—how the future movement in *OF* in Fig. 17 will be affected by the point on it at which trade is for the moment allowed to take place. A dynamic oligopoly problem is involved.

Before a tariff is actually imposed these matters would have to be given due weight. So would international external effects in production and consumption and all the considerations of strategy they involve. Moreover, in applying the formulæ of the preceding sections it must be borne in mind that domestic price-ratios are unlikely to reflect domestic rates of transformation and indifference, that protection may give birth to monopoly and disrupt domestic allocative efficiency, and that terminal foreign debt is unlikely to be independent of prices.

There are, finally, important administrative considerations. To give but a single example: the 'infant industry' argument for protection is properly based on the existence of external economies in domestic production, especially those operating through time. Instead of giving a subsidy (and so letting domestic price ratios reflect marginal rates of transformation) it may be simpler to impose a protective tariff—just as, on the grounds discussed in Chapter V, it may be more feasible to bring about a domestic redistribution of income by means of a tariff† than by theoretically perfect lump-sum measures. Any actual tariff will be imposed with all these matters in mind.

† There is an extensive literature on the actual effects of a tariff on the domestic distribution of income, but it belongs to positive (rather than to welfare or normative) economics.

APPENDIX TO CHAPTER IX

Let us maintain the convention that the services of productive factors are negative commodities, inputs negative outputs, and exports negative imports. Let us assume that production functions, both at home and abroad, are independent of the distribution of wealth; † and let us consider a domestic community of ν men, whose utility indexes take the form

$$u^\theta = u^\theta(x; y), \qquad (\theta = 1, \ldots, \nu) \tag{1}$$

where x and y are row vectors representing the amounts of the various goods going to the various men at home and abroad, respectively. Subscripts will refer to goods, superscripts to men. The number of foreigners will be written ν^*.

We have the two sets of equations

$$\left.\begin{aligned} \sum_\alpha x_i^\alpha &= X_i + z_i \\ \sum_\beta y_i^\beta &= Y_i - z_i \end{aligned}\right\} \qquad (i = 1, \ldots, n) \tag{2}$$

where X_i is the domestic production, Y_i the foreign production, and z_i the net import, of the ith good. Assuming that the horizon and the terminal capital equipment are given,‡ we have a domestic and a foreign production function. To allow for the possibility of international external effects in production, we shall (using vector notation) write these

$$T(X; Y) = 0 \tag{3}$$

and

$$T^*(X; Y) = 0, \tag{4}$$

respectively. Assuming, too, that we are told how much provision is to be made for foreign lending, we have the foreign trade transformation function

$$F(z) = 0, \tag{5}$$

which is specified more completely in the text.

† The reader will have no difficulty in allowing for this complication himself. It seems unnecessary to repeat the detailed treatment of the appendix to Chapter IV. I use the phrase 'production functions' rather than 'transformation functions' because the *foreign trade* transformation function, which depends on prices, is unlikely to be independent of the distribution of wealth.

‡ See Chapter VI. It is necessary that they be given both at home and abroad —unless there are no international external effects, in which case what happens abroad is irrelevant (cf. equation (9)).

The problem is to maximize, subject to (3), (4) and (5), *domestic* welfare: $W(u^1, \ldots, u^\nu)$. The first-order conditions can be written

$$\partial W/\partial x_i^\alpha + \lambda \partial T/\partial X_i + \lambda^* \partial T^*/\partial X_i = 0, \tag{6}$$

$$\partial W/\partial y_i^\beta + \lambda \partial T/\partial Y_i + \lambda^* \partial T^*/\partial Y_i = 0, \quad \begin{pmatrix} i = 1, \ldots, n \\ \alpha = 1, \ldots, \nu \\ \beta = 1, \ldots, \nu^* \end{pmatrix} \tag{7}$$

$$\partial W/\partial x_i^\alpha - \partial W/\partial y_i^\beta + \mu \partial F/\partial z_i = 0, \tag{8}$$

where λ, λ^* and μ are Lagrange multipliers. Provided we rule out excessive external effects in domestic consumption, the satisfaction of these equations will 'usually' lead to a maximum, rather than a minimum, of W.

If we assume (i) that domestic welfare is not directly affected by the consumption of foreigners, i.e. that there are no *international* external effects in consumption in this direction, and (ii) that there are no *international* external effects in production,† it follows immediately from (6) and (8) that

$$\frac{\partial W/\partial x_i^\alpha}{\partial W/\partial x_j^\theta} = \frac{\partial T/\partial X_i}{\partial T/\partial X_j} = \frac{\partial F/\partial z_i}{\partial F/\partial z_j}, \quad \begin{matrix} (i, j = 1, \ldots, n) \\ (\alpha, \theta = 1, \ldots, \nu) \end{matrix} \tag{9}$$

i.e. that marginal social rates of transformation in domestic factories must equal those through foreign trade, and that both must equal marginal social rates of indifference.

† Given that W is independent of y, it may at first sight appear sufficient to assume T^* independent of X; but this is not the case. Only when we assume both T^* independent of X and T independent of Y do the equations (7) become vacuous; and only when they become vacuous can we express (6)–(8) in the form of (9). If we fail to make both assumptions, (6)–(8) entail more than (9).

CHAPTER X

MARGINAL COST AND THE JUST PRICE

The measure of acceptance the marginal cost pricing principle has won among professional economists would be astonishing were not its pedigree so long and respectable.† A remarkable number do really seem to believe that public enterprises or nationalized industries should base their price and production policies on the principle or rule that *marginal cost should equal price*. The purpose of this chapter is to set out all the assumptions which have to be made if the rule is to be given a satisfactory welfare basis. An attempt will be made to distinguish those which relate to questions of *fact* from those which relate to articles of *faith*, and both from matters which are merely questions of *interpretation*.

Most of the assumptions are well known; and all have been encountered in the preceding chapters. But they are rarely stated in the literature, and it may assist in assessing the practical importance of the rule to have them set out with brief comments. It may also help the reader to appreciate why I shall suggest that the only price a public enterprise can be advised to set is what the medieval scholastics would have called the *pretium justum*.

DERIVATION OF THE MARGINAL COST 'RULE'

In what follows I shall leave till last the actual derivation of the rule that marginal cost should equal price. But in commenting

† The literature on this subject is large. At least four major streams in the history of recent economic thought converge upon it. There is the Marshall-Pigou discussion of the desirability of subsidizing decreasing cost industries and taxing increasing cost ones, and the prolonged controversy to which it gave rise. There is the literature on monopolistic and imperfect competition, and the divergence of monopoly output from competitive output. There is the work on the economic problems of socialism, dating back to Barone but recently associated with the names of Lange and Lerner. Finally, there is Professor Hotelling's fundamental paper (Harold Hotelling, 'The General Welfare in Relation to Problems of Taxation and of Railway and Utility Rates', *Econometrica*, vol. VI (1938), pp. 242–69) which takes as its starting-point the century-old contribution of Dupuit, and which has given rise to much discussion (both critical and uncritical) in the *Journal of Land and Public Utility Economics* (cf. 1942–4

on some of the assumptions underlying it I shall take its derivation for granted, so as to show how it would have to be modified if the assumption in question were to be relaxed.

(1) The first pair of assumptions constitute a basic article of faith: that individual preferences are to count—that preference maps are identical with welfare maps—and that a *cet. par.* increase in any one man's well-being increases social well-being. With these the reader is sufficiently familiar. The purist may care to add that there is the implied factual proposition that men have definite preference-scales. It is also worth recalling that the concept of welfare we have adopted is more appropriate *ex ante* than *ex post.*

(2) We assume that the location of the *horizon* is given, or agreed upon, so that the group in whose welfare we are interested is properly demarcated. Whether or not it is, is a question of fact.

(3) We assume that the items of *terminal capital equipment* are given or agreed upon. If they are not (or if people fail to agree on the proper location of the horizon), they may accept the rule that marginal cost should equal price, but hold widely divergent views on what marginal cost in fact is. This is because, before translation into monetary terms, a marginal cost is a marginal rate of transformation—and we cannot define marginal rates of transformation until the horizon and the terminal outputs of capital equipment are given.†

(4) We assume the absence of *risk and uncertainty*. If either is present—an 'if' which hardly requires factual investigation—it may occasionally be possible to find a consilience of opinion on the proper premium to add to (or subtract from) marginal cost. But it would be surprising if the benefits of the monopolist's quiet life (or the oligopolist's exciting one) could adequately be accounted for in this way. It would be even more surprising if the influence

issues, especially the articles by Troxel and Pegrum) and other journals. Detailed references to the main papers are to be found in two articles by Mrs Ruggles in the *Review of Economic Studies*, vol. XVII (1) and (2), 1949–50.

† Once the horizon is given, we can write the social transformation function $T(X_1,\dots,X_n;\, K_1,\dots,K_n)=0$. In it the X's are ordinary inputs and outputs and the K's items of terminal capital equipment. Marginal rates of transformation are typically $T_i(X;K)/T_j(X;K)$. They will clearly depend on the values we think it proper to attribute to the various K's.

of price-changes on anticipations of future income, and the effect of these anticipations on present welfare, could be accounted for. It seems fairly certain that once we allow factors other than the quantities of goods consumed and services rendered to have a direct influence on welfare, all the familiar marginal equivalences (of which the marginal cost rule is one) must be sacrificed in their entirety.

But if by chance people did agree on the proper way to adjust marginal costs and prices to allow for their direct influence on welfare through anticipations, there is a further (but minor) difficulty. Imperfect knowledge of what techniques will be available in the future, or of what inventions will occur—i.e. technological uncertainty—will make it extremely unlikely that people will agree on what marginal rates of transformation (and therefore marginal costs) really are.

(5) We assume that *the transformation functions are independent of the distribution of wealth*—another assumption of fact. If they are not and the consumption of a particular commodity (like meat or milk) has a marked effect on efficiency, it may be in accordance with the very general marginal equivalences of the General Optimum, set out in the appendix to Chapter IV, to price it well below marginal cost—or well above it, if (like gin) it is thought to reduce efficiency. Note that this has nothing whatever to do with external effects in either production or consumption. Note too that the change in consumption we desire for efficiency's sake may not be obtainable by a mere redistribution of wealth: the relevant income-elasticities of demand may be much smaller than the relevant price-elasticities. But if it is simply a case of workers being underfed, we may be able to save the marginal cost pricing principle by carrying out lump-sum redistributions of wealth in their favour.

(6) We assume *perfect divisibility*. This is in itself an assumption of fact; but it is so closely linked with the length of one of the slices of time we use in classifying commodities that value judgements are quite certainly involved. If significant indivisibilities exist among capital goods, the marginal cost curves relating to

final consumers' goods may be discontinuous. If they are, marginal cost is one thing for an expansion of output, and something else for a contraction. As we saw in Chapter VII, price should lie somewhere between the two extremes. But if the indivisibilities exist among final consumers' goods themselves, nothing can be saved of the marginal cost pricing principle. No necessary conditions for maximum welfare as general and all-embracing as the marginal equivalences of the General Optimum (of which the marginal cost rule is one) can be found. The attempts which have been made to find variants of the marginal cost pricing principle, applicable when these indivisibilities exist, are quite without foundation.†

(7) With the concept (or definition) of social welfare contained in (1), and the assumptions (2)–(6), we can (in the absence of excessive external effects in consumption) deduce the familiar marginal equivalences of the General Optimum as conditions necessary for the attainment of maximum welfare—i.e. for a maximum in terms of any Pareto W.‡ The equivalence basic to the marginal cost rule is the equality of marginal social rates of transformation and indifference. Just how it is basic will be revealed in due course. Here it is sufficient to emphasize that the necessary conditions for a maximum of welfare (and there may be several maxima in addition to the *maximum maximorum*) are also necessary for *minimum* welfare—and for stationary values. The adoption of the marginal cost pricing principle may lead to

† This goes for Professor Lewis's dictum that 'escapable' social cost should be covered. When indivisibilities exist among final consumers' goods, social cost can only be evaluated in terms of the specific value judgements of a well-defined W function. Cf. W. Arthur Lewis, *Overhead Costs* (London, 1949), Chaps. I, II.

Mr Fleming has recently tried to 'formulate the Hotelling-Lerner Rule of optimal output in the most general and least ambiguous way' (Marcus Fleming, 'Production and Price Policy in Public Enterprise', *Economica*, vol. XVII (1950), p. 1). He then proceeds to state a rule for *finite* movements—for which no rule exists. His attempted justification of the procedure in terms of consumers' and producers' surplus (ibid. p. 2) provides a striking example of the danger of using clumsy tools in delicate analysis (cf. Chapter VII). The only satisfactory justification is in terms of the explicit value judgement that the marginal social significance of money expenditure (no matter by whom expended) would be constant over the relevant range.

‡ It is unnecessary to repeat the process of deduction. The reader can refer to Chapter IV, or simply think of the tangency of the social production frontier with a social indifference curve of the Bergson frontier type.

one of these plateaux half-way up, a minor summit or the valley's bottom, just as easily as to the highest peak. Many positions on the ordinary slopes will be higher than many of the former. That is, many positions where marginal cost does not equal price may be better than many positions where it does.

As we saw in Chapter IV, the marginal equivalences of the General Optimum (and therefore the marginal cost pricing principle) are also necessary (but not sufficient) conditions for the attainment of the welfare frontier. Thus the adoption of the principle may just lead us to a position on the frontier which is neither an extremum nor a stationary value in terms of the *W* in which we are interested, but merely one of the infinity of positions from which it is impossible to move without making at least one member of the community worse off—i.e. merely one of the infinity of Pareto's *maxima d'utilité collective*. To this matter we return in (13).

(8) The marginal equivalences of the General Optimum are necessary conditions for maximum welfare only if satisfied *simultaneously*. Thus marginal cost should equal price in a particular industry only if the rule is *universally* applied. In particular, *it is not correct to say that marginal cost should equal price in a country which practises free trade*. Except in a degenerate case (where all the optimum taxes on imports and exports are zero) free trade involves the relaxation of the condition that marginal social rates of transformation through trade and in domestic factories be equal. The remaining conditions thereupon cease to be necessary for maximum welfare. To take an obvious example: welfare may be increased by the favourable movement in the terms of trade which could result from pricing domestically produced substitutes for imports below marginal cost, and exports above it.

Sometimes the necessity that the rule be universally applied is grudgingly conceded in the literature by stipulating that marginal cost should equal price in a particular industry only if 'competition is perfect elsewhere'. Even if we ignore foreign trade, external effects and various other complications, such a statement is loose and misleading. Unless the relative curvature of the transformation and indifference curves is 'right' (so that marginal cost curves rise, and indifference curves have the required convexity, in the neighbourhood of the optimum point), perfect competition may lead to minimum welfare—or to a stationary value, or minor maximum. This is particularly likely to happen when, because the relative curvature is 'wrong', the number of firms is wrong too. Then equating price to marginal cost in the existing firms may simply serve to worsen the existing mal-allocation of resources. A similar state of affairs will occur when too many, or too few, products are being produced. It is of course true that corrective taxes can right any degree of 'wrongness' in relative curvature which may exist; but they are unlikely to be feasible in practice. Whether the relative curvature is right or wrong is naturally a subject for empirical investigation. An armchair opinion is worthless.

(9) The next step is to identify social and private rates of indifference. This requires the factual assumption that external effects in consumption are non-existent (or that they fortuitously cancel out). Here an armchair opinion is not so worthless. It is clear from observation of the general process of taste formation in contemporary society that external effects are exceedingly important. Any pricing principle which ignores them has an exceedingly shaky foundation.

(10) Social and private rates of transformation are also identified. This is another assumption of fact. Perhaps it would be found more realistic than the corresponding one about consumption. But the external effects in production which operate through time —especially in connection with the training of a labour force (and therefore especially in new countries, developing areas or times of reconversion)—may well be considerable.

(11) The basic marginal equivalence now reads: marginal private rates of transformation and indifference should be equal. How do we translate this into 'marginal cost should equal price'?

(i) Firstly, we assume that each consumer will seek to achieve any given level of well-being in the cheapest possible way. (This is simply the assumption of utility maximization, stated in reverse.) It is well known that the equality of the ratios of marginal private costs (to individual consumers) and marginal private rates of indifference is entailed, except where a particular consumer does not consume a particular good at all. This proposition is usually stated in terms of *price-ratios* (not marginal cost ratios) *equalling private rates of indifference*; but that is because the case usually considered is where consumers trade at fixed market prices—i.e. where price and marginal cost coincide for any one consumer. For our purposes it is convenient to state the proposition in its most general form. (It is also convenient to interpret marginal revenue derived from the sale of productive services as negative marginal cost, so that the number of hours a man works is determined on the same basis as his purchases of consumption goods.)

(ii) Secondly, we assume that each producer will *produce any given output in the cheapest possible way*. It is a well known theorem in the theory of the firm that, when output is produced in the cheapest possible way, the marginal cost of output is equal to the marginal cost of any input multiplied by the marginal opportunity (or physical) cost of output in terms of that input. That is to say: the marginal cost of output is equal to the marginal cost of any input multiplied by the relevant marginal private rate of transformation. If the marginal cost of output is equated to its price, and if the producer buys inputs at fixed prices (so that marginal cost and price coincide for any input), we have *the equality of price ratios and marginal private rates of transformation*.†

† Let $C(x)$ be the total cost of producing output x, whose price is p_x, in a particular firm. Let p_i be the price, and y_i the quantity, of the ith input. Then $C = \Sigma p_i y_i$. Given x, we want to minimize C subject to the firm's production function: $x = f(y_1, \ldots, y_n)$. The first-order conditions are

$$1/\lambda = (p_i + a_i)/f_i, \tag{1}$$

where λ is a Lagrange multiplier and a_i is the amount by which the marginal cost of the ith input exceeds its price. That is to say: $(p_i + a_i)$ is the marginal cost of y_i. Now

$$\mathrm{d}x = \Sigma f_i\,\mathrm{d}y_i = \lambda\,\Sigma(p_i + a_i)\,\mathrm{d}y_i = \lambda\,\mathrm{d}C, \tag{2}$$

and so $1/\lambda = \mathrm{d}C/\mathrm{d}x$. Thus (1) yields

$$\mathrm{d}C/\mathrm{d}x = (p_i + a_i)/f_i. \tag{3}$$

If the marginal cost of output is equated to k-times its price, (3) yields

$$(p_i + a_i)/p_x = k f_i = k\,\partial x/\partial y_i. \tag{4}$$

When $k = 1$ and the a's are zero, (4) entails the equality of price-ratios and marginal private rates of transformation.

(iii) Finally, we assume that producers and consumers face the same fixed prices (or that they treat them as fixed, even if in fact they are not).† Then the equality of marginal private rates of transformation and indifference is secured. Both are equal to the fixed price ratios.

The immediately important assumption is of course the one contained in (ii)—that output is produced as cheaply as possible, inputs being valued at fixed prices. It is really part and parcel of the marginal cost pricing principle, and the two should always be mentioned in the same breath.‡

(12) It will be noted that the assumption of fixed (and therefore uniform) prices was introduced at a fairly late stage in both 11 (i) and 11 (ii). In strictness, the equality of marginal private rates of transformation can be achieved by securing the equality of price ratios for *marginal units* bought and sold by producers and consumers—that is, by securing the equality of marginal cost (or revenue) ratios. This may be done in two ways.

(i) It is conceivable that the degrees of monopoly and monopsony power may be the same for everyone, whether producer or consumer. Then marginal cost will diverge from price to exactly the same extent everywhere in the economy. If prices are uniform, so will marginal costs be. If private rates of transformation and indifference are equated to ratios of the latter, they too will be uniform and equal. This is conceivable, but extraordinarily unlikely: normally degrees of monopoly and monopsony power differ in *sign*. That is to say: marginal cost is usually above price, whereas marginal revenue is usually below it. If there is an imperfect market in selling, the development of imperfection in buying does not normally 'correct' matters; it aggravates the existing deviation

† The statement in the text is not completely accurate. A producer need not regard the price of his output (to which he equates marginal cost) as fixed. There is an asymmetry here, because the rule says 'equate marginal cost to price'—instead of 'to marginal revenue'.

‡ That is why Professor Lerner wisely states his rule in terms of applying more of an input whenever the value of its marginal product exceeds its price. This obviates the necessity of having *two* rules: 'equate marginal cost to price' and 'produce as cheaply as possible'. Cf. A. P. Lerner, *The Economics of Control* (New York, 1944), pp. 128 ff.

from ideal output. A hopelessly impracticable system of subsidies is required to achieve the correction.

(ii) The equality of price for marginal units can also be achieved under *discriminatory pricing*.† Provided that two consumers pay the same amount for, say, sugar *at the margin*, the marginal equivalences of the General Optimum are unaffected by what they pay for the intramarginal units. That affects the *distribution of wealth*, and nothing else—it affects the position attained on the welfare frontier, but not the actual attainment of the frontier. It would of course be extraordinarily hard to discriminate so perfectly that each man had to pay the same price for a marginal purchase, and discriminatory pricing is in practice bound to lead to a disruption of the marginal equivalences.

(13) The last, and perhaps the most important, assumption required for the validity of the marginal cost pricing principle will now be clear. We must assume that *the distribution of wealth to which it leads is approved*. Under the conditions we have set out, the adoption of the principle will lead to the welfare frontier. But it need not lead to the most favoured point on the frontier (where a *W* contour just touches it: cf. Fig. 9*b*). Lump-sum taxes and bounties are required to secure the desired movement along the frontier. If they are infeasible, it may be wise to sacrifice the marginal cost principle. Many positions inside the welfare frontier will represent higher social welfare than many positions actually on the frontier. To this matter we return.

(14) I turn now to a problem of interpretation which has caused much confusion in the literature. Are the marginal costs to which prices should be equated long-period ones or short-period ones? The problem is resolved when we recall that there is only one kind

† Discrimination occurs whenever different units of the same commodity are bought (or sold) at different prices from (or to) different people, or for different uses. Note that if a doctor charges different patients different fees for the same operation, it does *not* constitute discrimination in the above sense. Operations performed on different patients may be perfect substitutes from the doctor's viewpoint, but they are not as far as the patients are concerned. They do not, therefore, comprise a homogeneous commodity. On the other hand, bottles of the same medicine sold to different patients do comprise a homogeneous commodity. Patients can exchange bottles of medicine. They cannot exchange operations.

of marginal cost in our system of analysis: that relating to one of the slices of time used in the classification of commodities. *Price should equal marginal cost in each slice*—or 'for each commodity', if we adhere to the rule that physically identical goods relating to different slices are different commodities.

Probably the confusion in the literature has arisen because the majority of writers are unwilling to accept anything as unrealistic as a division of time into a succession of slices—even if they are not unwilling to divide the continuous range of contemporaneous goods into a finite number of homogeneous commodities. If we let the length of the slice tend to zero, it is clear that *price should equal instantaneous marginal cost, and vary with it*.† But most economists would want to say that continuous price changes were 'a nuisance', and that a compromise should be struck. So it probably should. But definite value judgements are required in matters of this sort—just as they are required in deciding upon a classification of commodities (and the length of the slices) in the first place. What started as a problem of interpretation soon involves articles of faith.

(15) Another problem of interpretation is the following. We have established that *equating* price to marginal cost will lead to the satisfaction of one of the necessary conditions for maximum welfare. Until quite recently it was thought that securing the *proportionality* of prices and marginal costs would do equally well.‡ This view is no longer held, but it is instructive to see in what circumstances it would be correct. Assume that marginal cost is everywhere k-times price. A glance at the preceding mathematical footnote reveals that the price ratios between inputs and outputs will then be k-times the relevant marginal private rates of transformation. Now if the inputs are commodities bought or sold by consumers (e.g. coal or labour), these price ratios will still be equal to the private rates of indifference, which will therefore diverge

† Taking a fairly short slice provides the basis for differentiating between peak and off-peak charges for electricity. Cf. W. Arthur Lewis, *Overhead Costs* (London, 1949), Chap. II.

‡ Probably the first writer to question the 'proportionality rule' was A. Bergson, *The Structure of Soviet Wages* (Cambridge, Mass., 1944), pp. 19–22.

from the private rates of transformation. Proportionality is thus generally insufficient—equality must be sought. But there are three exceptions:

(i) If none of the inputs enter consumers' preference-scales, the price ratios between inputs and outputs will not affect consumers in any way. (The price ratios between different outputs still will, but their equality with rates of transformation and indifference is not destroyed by the proportionality of prices to marginal costs.) Sometimes this condition is phrased: all the factors of production must be in completely inelastic supply and indifferent between the various uses to which they can be put.† There is nothing wrong with this formulation, but it is apt to lead to the definitely misleading statement that proportionality is sufficient 'if the hours of work are fixed'. If men are not indifferent between various kinds of work (and here I do *not* mean *indifferent at the margin*), or if inputs other than labour (e.g. coal or gas) enter their preference-scales, fixing the number of hours worked is irrelevant.

(ii) If all the inputs which enter consumers' preference-scales are taxed, a divergence between price and marginal cost may be called for. The simplest case to consider is where the marginal rate of income-tax is the same for all men, and where labour is the only input which enters their preference-scales. It is straightforward to show that prices should then be equated to *marginal cost* × (1 − *the marginal rate of income-tax*).‡ If other inputs do enter preference-scales, their use in production should be taxed at the same rate

† Cf. P. A. Samuelson, *Foundations of Economic Analysis* (Cambridge, Mass., 1947), pp. 240 and 253.

‡ Consider for simplicity a consumer who consumes x and renders the productive service y. The prices of x and y are p_x and p_y. His utility function is $U(x, y)$, which he tries to maximize subject to the budgetary constraint

$$p_x \cdot x = \phi(p_y \cdot y),$$

where $\phi(p_y \cdot y)$ is his income after tax. The first-order condition may be written

$$\frac{U_x}{U_y} = -\frac{p_x}{p_y \phi'}.$$

If marginal private rates of indifference and transformation are to be equal, reference to the preceding mathematical footnote (p. 148) reveals that the k in equation (4) must be set equal to $1/\phi'$. Then price is ϕ'-times marginal cost. But $(1-\phi')$ is the marginal rate of income-tax. This proves the statement in the text.

as leisure. Perhaps it is easiest to see this by reflecting that, if the marginal rate of income-tax is one-third, a firm has to pay £3 for £2's worth of a consumer's leisure. It should therefore also pay £3 for £2's worth of coal—or whatever other input enters preference-scales. And it should price its output at two-thirds of marginal cost.

(iii) If all final consumers' goods are subject to purchase-tax at the same marginal rate, price should be equated to marginal cost divided by (1 + *the marginal rate of tax*). This does not require separate discussion.

(16) The concept of welfare we have adopted attributes direct welfare significance to quantities of final consumers' goods produced, productive services rendered by consumers, and nothing else. How *intermediate* goods (i.e. producers' goods) are priced is of no direct consequence. But it requires no more than a simple application of the law of derived demand to show that, if they too are priced at marginal cost, the whole chain of marginal equivalences, from inputs of productive services to outputs of final consumers' goods, will be satisfied.

A difficulty does however arise if (because an income-tax exists, or for some other reason) prices are merely proportional to marginal costs. Let us suppose that they should be half the latter, on the assumption that production is carried out in one stage. Now if in some parts of the economy production is carried out in two stages, between which the unfinished goods pass through the market, it is clearly wrong to set price at one-half of marginal cost in *both* stages—for the final price would then be a fourth of the original marginal cost. An exceedingly complicated set of pricing 'rules' is required to cope with the complications to which a realistic multiplicity of stages would certainly give rise.

(17) There is a final matter of interpretation. The marginal cost principle refers to the pricing of goods which can be produced. It says nothing about the pricing of goods in completely inelastic supply. They can be priced at whatever level one pleases. If there are no external effects in consumption, if the goods are perfectly divisible, and if one approves of the distribution of

wealth and accepts consumers' preferences, that level will presumably be the one which equates demand and supply. If one of these conditions is not fulfilled, discriminatory prices, rationing and free (or compulsory) distribution of the goods may have a part to play—and this, of course, is true whether or not supply is completely inelastic.

THE JUST PRICE

It seems fairly clear that the conditions which have to be met before it is correct (from a welfare viewpoint) to set price equal to marginal cost in a particular industry are so restrictive that they are unlikely to be satisfied in practice. The survival of the marginal cost pricing principle is probably no more than an indication of the extent to which the majority of professional economists are ignorant of the assumptions required for its validity. How else can one account for the glib advocacy of the principle in a society where the marginal rate of income-tax is certainly not zero, where optimum taxes are certainly not imposed on both imports and exports, where external effects in consumption are of the first importance, where uncertainty and expectation play a major role in making life worth living, where . . . ?

Occasionally one encounters the argument that, even if the assumptions underlying the marginal cost principle are rather unrealistic, it can at least be used as a *basis*. Then prices can be raised a little where external diseconomies in production or consumption are thought to be important, lowered where consumption of the good in question is likely to increase efficiency, and so on. No doubt this is more reasonable. But why not take some other price as a basis? The assumptions which would have to be made to prove that price should be k-times *average* cost (or the square root of average cost) are not much more unrealistic than those required for proving that it should equal marginal cost. If a basis is all that we are looking for, we may as well start with all prices zero.

But to my mind the cardinal objection lies deeper. Any principle we formulate as a special case of one of the marginal equivalences of the General Optimum will, on the usual assumptions, take us to the welfare frontier. That is half the battle won, but only half. We also want a particular distribution of wealth. If lump-sum measures were feasible, they could move us along the frontier to the point we most desired. We saw in Chapter V, however, that lump-sum redistributions of wealth are almost certainly not feasible. By far the simplest way of securing the distribution of wealth we desire is *through the price system*. In this I include income-taxes, which affect the price of labour (or leisure). Much of orthodox welfare theory lacks realism precisely because it assumes that the desired distribution of wealth has already been attained (and is somehow maintained), and then proceeds to regard the price system as a highly specialized resource-allocating mechanism which exercises no influence whatever on the distribution of wealth. Such a view is not easy to defend.

I suggest that the only price a public enterprise or nationalized industry can be expected to set is what we may as well call a *just price—a price which is set with some regard for its effect on the distribution of wealth* as well as for its effect on the allocation of resources. Definite value judgements are naturally required for its determination—and a good deal of positive knowledge. In the final chapter I shall develop the theme that the task of the economist is to provide the positive knowledge, not to recommend the level at which price should be set.

CHAPTER XI

SOCIAL INCOME AND INDEX NUMBERS

The problem of the evaluation of 'real' national income has recently received considerable attention. Hicks,† Kuznets,‡ Little § and Samuelson || have made significant alterations to the foundations laid by Pigou.¶ The purpose of this chapter is to survey the ground fairly rapidly and to examine some of the interpretations which have been suggested for index numbers of the type the national income statisticians habitually construct.

INTERTEMPORAL COMPARISONS OF WELL-BEING

In Chapter V we discussed in a 'comparative-statical' way the effect of a given change on welfare. That is, we did not try to compare welfare in one period with welfare in another period. We asked instead what would happen to welfare *in a given period* if some hypothetical change were made. We were concerned with *contemporaneous* comparisons. We saw that the problem can be tackled quite directly whenever we are given a well-defined W, but that we have to content ourselves with occasional statements, based on shifts in efficiency loci, about potential welfare (or 'potential desirability') whenever we know no more than that W is a Paretian welfare function.

Very much the same applies when we turn to consider intertemporal comparisons of well-being—comparisons of welfare in one period (or 'year') with welfare in another. But some additional complications arise. These can be made to stand out most clearly

† J. R. Hicks, 'The Valuation of Social Income', *Economica*, vol. VII (1940), pp. 105–24; *idem*, 'The Valuation of Social Income—A Comment on Professor Kuznets's Reflections', *Economica*, vol. XV (1948), pp. 163–72.

‡ Simon Kuznets, 'On the Valuation of Social Income—Reflections on Professor Hicks's Article', *Economica*, vol. XV (1948), pp. 1–16 and 116–31.

§ I. M. D. Little, 'The Valuation of Social Income', *Economica*, vol. XVI (1949), pp. 11–26; *idem*, 'A Note on the Interpretation of Index Numbers', *Economica*, vol. XVI (1949), pp. 369–70.

|| Paul A. Samuelson, 'Evaluation of Real National Income', *Oxford Economic Papers*, New Series, vol. II (1950), pp. 1–29.

¶ A. C. Pigou, *The Economics of Welfare* (4th ed., London, 1932), Part I.

if we start with a very formal analysis of the case where we actually have a well-defined W. This is given in (1) below. (2) discusses the case where W is only known to be Paretian. In other respects there is little to add to the analysis of Chapter V.

(1) Since we are comparing two years, we have two distinct horizons demarcating two distinct groups. Of course, the groups will probably overlap; and (if no births or deaths occur) they may even coincide—but that is unlikely. Let us assume that the men comprising the first group are numbered 1, ..., α; and those comprising the second, β, ..., ν. If there is an overlap, β will be less than α; if the two groups coincide, we will have $\beta=1$ and $\nu=\alpha$. Assuming for the moment that tastes remain unchanged from the one year to the other, we can write the utility indicators of the various men $(u^1, ..., u^\nu)$, and the social welfare function $W(u^1, ..., u^\nu)$, as before. Then welfare in the first year is

$$W_1 = W(u_1^1, \ldots, u_1^\beta, \ldots, u_1^\alpha, 0, \ldots, 0),$$

and welfare in the second year is

$$W_2 = W(0, \ldots, 0, u_2^\beta, \ldots, u_2^\alpha, \ldots, u_2^\nu),$$

if we adopt the convention that a man enjoys zero well-being when he does not belong to the group.† Whether or not welfare is said to increase will depend on whether or not $W_2 > W_1$.

Stating the problem in this very formal way has several advantages. Consider first what happens if the tastes of some of the men who belong to both groups do not remain unchanged. Since W is defined with reference to a particular set of utility functions, it must be redefined if any one of them changes. Let us suppose that it is W^* on the basis of the first year's tastes, and W^{**} on the basis of the second year's. There are now two distinct possibilities. If the ethical beliefs defining the W's are such that they have *cardinal* significance, we can say that welfare has increased whenever $W_2^{**} > W_1^*$. But if the W's have only *ordinal* significance,

† Note that this is a pure convention. Any other number would do equally well. Note too that it is not sufficient to put the amounts of goods purchased and services rendered all equal to zero in a utility function when the man to which it refers does not belong to the group, for that would imply that he enjoyed a year's leisure.

we can do no more than compare the two years first on the basis of the one's tastes, and then on the basis of the other's. It may easily happen that $W_2^{**} > W_1^{**}$ and $W_2^{*} < W_1^{*}$, so that we have an ambiguity. This is one of the few instances I have been able to discover where a cardinal social welfare function has advantages over an ordinal one.†

Ignoring changing tastes, the rigid formality of the analysis brings out very clearly the fact that *additional* value judgements (i.e. ones additional to those implied by the definition of the W's we have hitherto been using) are required to evaluate the contribution which *savings* make to social welfare. Normally the u's in a W are assumed to depend on quantities of goods consumed and services rendered, and nothing else. We saw in Chapter VI that we could allow them to depend also on the amounts of the various items of terminal capital equipment—if we are prepared to let all institutional factors affecting the productivity of capital play a direct part in determining welfare (which means that we must be prepared to sacrifice, as necessary conditions for maximum welfare, all the marginal equivalences on which some welfare theorists lay such stress). But savings (whether personal or collective) fit very uncomfortably into the usual framework. It is not easy to make allowance for the degree of security they undoubtedly provide—just as it is not easy to make allowance for the effect on present welfare of anticipations, and the confidence with which they are held. To take factors such as these into account we must make additional value judgements—and they are likely to be value judgements on which agreement will be difficult to reach.‡

(2) Let us now consider the case where W is not clearly defined, but is merely known to be Paretian. As in Chapter V, we can only speak of *potential* welfare—and of that only when the now familiar difficulties about savings and terminal capital have

† Another instance is where we want to say that the *change* in welfare over one period is greater than the *change* over a second.

‡ This remark has a bearing on the controversy between Professor Kuznets and Dr Little regarding the correct method of proceeding once the field of current consumption is left. Cf. I. M. D. Little, 'The valuation of Social Income', *Economica*, vol. XVI (1949), pp. 23–5; and S. Kuznets, 'On the Valuation of Social Income', *Economica*, vol. XV (1948), pp. 12–16.

been satisfactorily resolved. Moreover, since we can only speak of potential welfare on the basis of shifts in efficiency loci, ambiguities may arise whenever the group changes its composition. We may find that the first group would be potentially better off in the one year, and the second group in the other.

Assuming for the moment that the two groups coincide, a further difficulty arises whenever tastes change. For it seems clear that we must recognize that a man's tastes in the second year will normally depend on what he has consumed in the past—and in particular on what he consumed in the first year. To accept present (or any other) tastes as data, and to base statements about potential welfare upon them, is to give our approval to the historical pattern of consumption. It is always open for someone to argue that present tastes would be different if only wealth had been 'properly' distributed in the past, and that any alleged increase in potential welfare would disappear if the appropriate correction were made. To be beyond criticism on this score we must never say that there has been a potential increase in welfare between one year and another unless we can be sure that the observed shift in the efficiency locus would not be reversed by any hypothetical historical redistributions of wealth. That is asking quite a lot.

INDEX NUMBERS

It is evident that we will not be able to attach much welfare significance to ordinary index numbers of output or consumption if we maintain the purism of the last section. Referring only to aggregates, and weighted by prices which rule under a particular distribution of wealth, they are neither sufficiently detailed to tell us what that distribution is nor sufficiently general to have much relevance for other distributions. They give no information about changes in tastes, or in the composition of the group; and—though this is a minor point, easily remedied—they normally take no account of changes in the amount of work performed.

Various interpretations of index numbers have nevertheless been attempted, and some of them are valid and useful if the appropriate simplifying assumptions are granted. Those examined below do not deal specifically with the subtle complications which arise in connection with intertemporal comparisons of welfare, and are perhaps best regarded as exercises in contemporaneous comparison—although their originators seem to have claimed rather more for them.

(1) In 1940 Professor Hicks proved the following theorem,† in which the p's refer to market prices, the q's to aggregate quantities, and the subscripts 1 and 2 to the 'years' involved. The *Hicks theorem* states:

If (i) The group remains unchanged,
(ii) tastes remain unchanged (and are independent of prices),
(iii) there are no external effects in consumption,
(iv) individual indifference curves are convex to the origin,
(v) consumers trade at fixed prices, which equate demand and supply,

then

$$\Sigma p_2 q_2 \geqslant \Sigma p_2 q_1$$

entails that the exchange-economy welfare frontier ‡ of the second year lies outside that of the first year in the neighbourhood of the position actually observed in the second year. That is to say: without destroying the equality of marginal rates of indifference, it is possible so to redistribute the first year's collection of goods that everybody is worse off than in the second year; or, putting it the other way round, it is *not* possible so to redistribute the first year's goods that everyone is better off than in the second year.

† J. R. Hicks, 'The Valuation of Social Income', *Economica*, vol. VII (1940), pp. 111 ff. A fuller statement of the proof is contained in P. A. Samuelson, 'Evaluation of Real National Income', *Oxford Economic Papers*, New Series, vol. II (1950), pp. 7–9. The statement of the theorem given in the text makes explicit a number of assumptions inherent in Professor Hicks's treatment. The validity of the conclusion is destroyed when any one of them is relaxed, and it is difficult to know how to interpret his remark, made in reply to Professor Kuznets's 'Reflections': 'I should always have admitted that population changes had to be allowed for' ('The Valuation of Social Income—A Comment on Professor Kuznets's Reflections', *Economica*, vol. XV (1948), p. 163). The reader will search in vain for an indication of the way in which the allowing is to be done, or what would remain of the theorem once the admission were made.

‡ See Chapter IV. An 'exchange-economy welfare frontier' is an ordinary welfare frontier drawn up with a *fixed* collection of goods. Note that assumptions (iii)–(v) entail that society is actually 'on' the frontier.

For a proof of this elegant result the reader is referred to the literature. Professor Hicks originally used it as a translation into index number form of his basic 'compensation test' for an increase in social income (which we examined in Chapter V).† Since we found reasons for rejecting the test itself, we can hardly agree to its use in providing a simple welfare interpretation for the index number inequality—even in the unlikely event of the assumptions (i)–(v) being satisfied. The theorem is mentioned in this context simply because it has been taken over by Dr Little, to whose criterion we must now turn.

(2) We saw in Chapter V that Dr Little's double criterion for an increase in welfare, while formally valid, is not very useful. The criterion is: ‡ Welfare (or 'real income') increases between the two years if (*a*) the distribution of welfare is no worse, and (*b*) the first year's collection of goods cannot be so redistributed that everyone is better off than in the second year. Now, if the assumptions underlying the Hicks theorem are granted, $\Sigma p_2 q_2 \geqslant \Sigma p_2 q_1$ implies that (*b*) is satisfied. Thus, if this inequality holds and a man agrees that the distribution of welfare has not changed for the worse, he must (on Dr Little's criterion) agree that welfare (or 'real income') has increased.

The reason why the criterion does not seem to be very useful is that Dr Little uses the expression 'the distribution is no worse' in a rather curious way.§ Let us refer to the position in the second year as II, to that in the first as I, and to that resulting when the first's goods are so redistributed (by lump-sum measures) that everyone is worse off than in II as I'. (That is, I' lies on the exchange-economy welfare frontier passing through I, and is south-west of II.) Now when Dr Little says that the distribution at II is no worse than that at I, he means $W(I') \geqslant W(I)$. He uses I' as an intermediate point, and asks us to judge its welfare. If we

† In Chapter V we phrased the test in terms of efficiency loci. Whether they, exchange-economy welfare frontiers or true (production-economy) welfare frontiers are the most appropriate is a matter for individual judgement.

‡ Cf. I. M. D. Little, 'The Valuation of Social Income', *Economica*, vol. XVI (1949), pp. 369–70. I have benefited greatly from a prolonged correspondence with Dr Little on this matter.

§ Cf. the discussion in Chapter V.

agree that it is better than I, we must agree that II is still better—for everyone is better off in II than in I'. It seems more sensible, however, to ask quite directly whether or not $W(II) > W(I)$. The use of an intermediate point I', to the south-west of II, is not very helpful—especially since we do not actually experience it, and are therefore less likely to be willing to judge its welfare than the welfare of I or II (which we do experience).

The only role the index number inequality plays in the process is to assure us that a point I', south-west of II, *can* be attained with the first year's collection of goods without destroying the equality of marginal rates of indifference. This is not a very important role, and it is doubtful if it can be regarded as a satisfactory basis for 'interpreting' index numbers. There is no reason why, if we are going to make any judgements at all in terms of a W, we should not compare $W(I)$ and $W(II)$ quite directly, without worrying about either I' or the index number inequality.

(3) Professor Samuelson has recently put forward an interpretation for index numbers which I believe to be erroneous in a strictly formal sense. He states the theorem:† 'Where playing the game of perfect competition can be depended to follow the invisible hand to bliss' (i.e. where there are no external effects, individual indifference curves are convex to the origin, diminishing returns prevail and prices equal marginal costs), $\Sigma p_2 q_2 > \Sigma p_2 q_1$ entails a higher W in year 2 than in year 1 *provided the distribution of income is optimal in both years*—i.e. provided W is at a constrained maximum in both years.‡

It could justly be remarked that the assumption that the distribution is optimal is rather 'like saying I must always want to be in the town in which I am, even if I happen to be motoring rapidly through it';§ but it is an assumption which will un-

† P. A. Samuelson, 'Evaluation of Real National Income', *Oxford Economic Papers*, New Series, vol. II (1950), pp. 28–9. In private correspondence Professor Samuelson has agreed that the theorem is invalid.

‡ In point of fact, if the theorem were true at all, it would suffice for the distribution to be optimal in the second year.

§ I. M. D. Little, 'The Foundations of Welfare Economics', *Oxford Economic Papers*, New Series, vol. I (1949), pp. 237–8.

doubtedly appeal to many who are content to discuss the behaviour of welfare frontiers as though the economies to which they referred were in fact optimally organized. The theorem is therefore worth examining.

The proof Professor Samuelson suggests may be followed in Fig. 18. The amounts of two outputs, X and Y, are measured along the axes. T_2T_2 is the second year's social transformation function, showing the combinations in which the two goods are available to the community. $\bar{B}$ and $\bar{\bar{B}}$ are two social indifference curves of the Bergson frontier type, showing the combinations of X and Y which represent (when all optimal arrangements have been made) the same social income in terms of a given W. The situation actually observed in the second year is A (where $\bar{B}$ just touches T_2T_2); in the first year it is C. NN is the price-line, tangential (under the assumed conditions) to both T_2T_2 and $\bar{B}$. $\Sigma p_2q_2 > \Sigma p_2q_1$ clearly implies that C lies beneath NN. If the Bergson frontiers are convex to the origin, like ordinary indifference curves, C must lie beneath $\bar{B}$ too. The theorem follows.

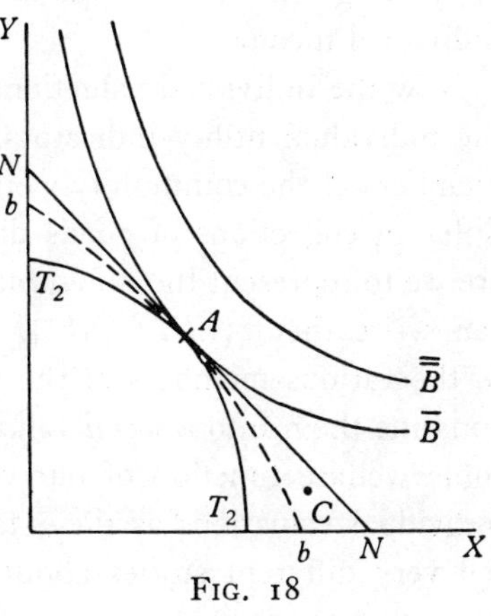

FIG. 18

The crucial factor is obviously the convexity to the origin of the Bergson frontiers. Professor Samuelson seems to regard convexity as the 'normal' case. But, as we saw in Chapter III, there is no reason why Bergson frontiers should not be concave, even if the individual indifference curves out of which they are constructed have the conventional convexity. We cannot, therefore, rule out the possibility of the Bergson frontiers being shaped like the dotted *bb* curve in the diagram; and, when they are thus shaped, the theorem is false.

A SUGGESTED INTERPRETATION

Hitherto our approach to the problem of social valuation has been based on each man valuing that part of the social income which accrues to him (whether or not his valuation is affected by what accrues to others—i.e. whether or not there are external effects in consumption). There is, however, no reason why we should not let each man value instead the whole social income, taking into account both its distribution and its composition. Then the problem of social valuation is that of 'weighing' the individual valuations of social income against one another, rather than that of 'adding' (in terms of some *W*) the individual valuations of individual income.

Now the individual valuations of individual income are simply the individual utility indicators, which indicate how the various members of the community would choose between (or 'vote for') different collections of goods distributed in different ways. How are we to represent the individual valuations of *social* income? We can write them $\{W^1, ..., W^\nu\}$, where the various *W*'s appertain to the various members of the community. We can (if we wish) combine them into a *social* valuation of social income in terms of some welfare function of our own; or we can simply leave the individual valuations as they stand and recognize that they may tell very different stories about the movement in social income between two years.

If all the members of the community accept the basic Paretian value judgements, so that each man is prepared to let the preferences of his fellows 'count', the *W*'s representing individual valuations of social income will all be Pareto *W*'s. It will, as we saw in Chapter V, then be impossible to draw a distinction between the 'size' and the 'distribution' of the national income, and to say that welfare depends on them both. Yet the majority of men do seem to use something like the analogy of 'the national cake and its slices' when comparing two social incomes, and so it seems that at least some of the *W*'s will be non-Paretian. Nor is this very surprising. Let us see why.

There is no obvious reason why anyone should want individual preferences to 'count' where *intertemporal* comparisons of well-being are concerned. The purpose of letting them 'count' for contemporaneous comparisons is presumably to ensure that society will not choose what each one of its members would want it to reject. But there is no real possibility of choice between this year's income and last year's. Both are accomplished facts. You cannot make time reversible and choose between them. The most you can do is to say which, in retrospect, seems to have been the better year. There is no reason why your retrospection should pay particular regard to the preferences of others (which in any case you will not know). It can be as paternalistic as you please.

If this much is granted, and if it is agreed that a man asked 'Is welfare greater than last year?' is unlikely to try to 'add' (in terms of his private Pareto *W*) the various changes in individual well-being which have occurred (even if he knows what they are), but is much more likely to try to form some crude idea of whether or not there has been an 'improvement' in his opinion—perhaps using some equally crude 'size-distribution' dichotomy—the role of index numbers appears in a new light. The role of an index of aggregate output or consumption is simply to provide him with a certain amount of information to help him form a balanced judgement on the relative merits of two years. If we like, we can think of it as *some* sort of index of the 'size' of the national income (for it is abundantly clear that it can tell us nothing about its 'distribution')—but there is no need to insist on such an interpretation. Where practicable, however, index numbers of aggregate output or consumption should always be supplemented with information about the distribution of income and wealth—and also with separate indexes of investment, personal and collective savings, and expenditure on collective goods like defence. The more information made available, the more likely is it that a balanced judgement will be obtained.

It is, on this view, really important to see that the index numbers we construct do provide as much information as possible. The weights used in their construction should therefore be widely known or readily ascertainable. For this reason it seems evident that weighting quantities by *current* prices, which people are likely to know, is more useful than weighting them by the prices which ruled in some distant base year, and are but dimly recalled by the oldest inhabitants. If this is done it is reasonable to hope that 'what the index numbers mean' will become more widely understood—much more so than would result from making wildly improbable assumptions (such as 'all men are alike', 'population and tastes remain unchanged', 'the distribution is optimal', or 'there are no external effects in consumption') and trying to evolve some sort of utilitarian interpretation.

If we are prepared to accept a valuation of 1949 income at 1936 prices as a useful piece of information *in its own right*—and a valuation in terms of more recent prices as a piece more useful still—we need not, as economists, go on to draw welfare conclusions. That each man can be left to do for himself, according to his own lights, and making use of whatever other information is available to him. The chief error of those who have attempted definite welfare interpretations of index numbers is simply that they have expected too much.

It is tempting to conclude with the remark that the way of looking at index numbers outlined above is not only a fairly sensible one, but is in fact the one the majority of economists do use in the ordinary course of their work. It is only in the hands of sophisticated theoreticians that index numbers become more than useful bits of data, and are asked to carry meanings they cannot be expected to bear.

CHAPTER XII

CONCLUSION

The purpose of theoretical welfare economics, as developed in the preceding chapters, is largely to see that *specific* injunctions can be deduced from *general* premisses—that is, from premisses that are widely accepted. The injunctions must be fairly specific if they are to be of any interest—it would not help much to be told that the price of coal should lie somewhere between zero and plus infinity. And the premisses must command wide acceptance, for otherwise the injunctions they entail would hardly be worth deducing.

Now, broadly speaking, widely accepted premisses are of two kinds: factual and ethical. There is no need to go into the subtle philosophical points involved in distinguishing the one from the other, but perhaps an example will help to make the distinction sufficiently clear. I have consistently referred to interpersonal comparisons of well-being as questions of ethics rather than questions of fact. What that means is this. If two people disagree on the contributions which various levels of individual well-being make to social well-being, it is extraordinarily hard to think of some objective test which would settle the matter to the satisfaction of both. The question is therefore an ethical one. If, however, two people disagreed on the relative weights of two physical objects, it is extremely probable that they would abide by the verdict of a pair of scales. The question is therefore one of fact.

The important thing to notice about the above example is that the decision to abide by the verdict of a pair of scales—or of any other 'objective' test—is itself in the last resort an act of faith, based on fundamentally ethical notions. So we have really done no more than push the problem of distinguishing the factual from the ethical one stage further back. But, instead of pursuing it all the way to the realm of metaphysics, it is sufficient to remark that more people would probably agree on the dividing line between the factual and the ethical, or on what constitutes an 'objective' test and what does not, than would agree on the ethical matters themselves.†

The question of agreement is really fundamental. Let us take it for granted that wide, if not universal, agreement can be obtained on the factual assumptions underlying welfare theory. The possibility of building an interesting theory then hinges on the possibility of obtaining a sufficient consilience of opinion on ethical matters to enable specific injunctions to be deduced. Now, clearly, there is some degree of consilience of opinion in any reasonably homogeneous society—indeed, one might almost claim that, if a society is to cohere at all, at least a majority of its members must share some basic articles of faith. But whether or not the common ground is sufficiently extensive for the purposes of welfare theory is another matter.

It is sometimes suggested ‡ that there is in fact a comprehensive enough consensus of opinion on ends, or on essentially ethical matters, to give welfare theory some scope. Thus it may be argued that there is today almost universal agreement on the desirability of full employment, the necessity of maintaining a reasonably stable level of prices, or of solving the dollar crisis. But it does not seem to be realized how *detailed* the agreement on ends must be if a consistent theory of welfare economics is to be erected. There are an infinite number of policy combinations capable (in theory) of securing full employment. No two will have precisely similar effects on all the variables which influence welfare. How are we to choose between them? I doubt if any two people really agree in

† Thus the consilience of opinion necessary for the pursuit of positive studies is much more likely to be obtained than that necessary for the pursuit of normative studies.

‡ Cf. G. J. Stigler, 'The New Welfare Economics', *American Economic Review*, vol. XXXIII (1943), pp. 355–9. See also P. A. Samuelson, 'Further Commentary on Welfare Economics', *American Economic Review*, vol. XXXIII (1943), pp. 604–7. It was, I think, in this controversy that the terms 'New' and 'Old' Welfare Economics came into being—the difference between the two allegedly being that the former does not involve interpersonal comparisons (once the group is demarcated?), whereas the latter does. It seems to me that the distinction is somewhat overdrawn. It is all really just a matter of how completely or incompletely the W function is defined. If we know no more than that it is Paretian, we have to speak 'New Welfare Economics'; if we do know more than that, we can speak 'Old Welfare Economics' whenever we want to.

detail on the best way of securing full employment, no matter how many may agree that it should be secured.

We have seen that, to build even the elements of a theory of welfare along the conventional lines, we must have agreement on the horizon (which demarcates the group of men in whose welfare we are interested), on such specific matters as the items of terminal capital equipment (which together play an important role in determining the general rate of economic 'progress') and the 'correct' attitude to uncertainty. It seems to me extremely improbable that agreement on these basic matters will ever be obtained. And it seems to me, therefore, that the possibility of building a useful and interesting theory of welfare economics—i.e. one which consists of something more than the barren formalisms typified by the marginal equivalences of conventional theory—is exceedingly small.

I feel that the real difficulty which any individualist theory of welfare has to face lies in these basic assumptions rather than, as seems to be popularly supposed, in making interpersonal comparisons. It is of course true that the majority of policies which welfare theory has to appraise will involve redistributional changes of some magnitude, and that interpersonal comparisons are required. But I suspect that a surprising degree of agreement on whether a given redistribution is good or bad will often be found in contemporary Western society. Equalitarian ideals, with money income (or, perhaps, wealth valued in monetary terms) as the yardstick of equality, are nowadays extraordinarily widely dispersed.

Be that as it may, another major difficulty which an individualist theory of welfare has to face is not at the ethical level at all. I refer to the existence of external effects in consumption. This is a simple factual matter, on which disagreement is unlikely to be marked. We have simply to pose the question: Are a man's choices (of items of personal consumption) influenced by the consumption-patterns, past or present, of other men? I do not think there can be much doubt that they are—and very markedly, too. Any satisfactory individualist theory of welfare must, therefore take this fact into account. It is here that the major difficulty arises. A theory which takes external effects in consumption into account seems to become so hopelessly complicated that any chance of ever applying it becomes exceedingly remote. Much of the appeal of what we might call *laissez-faire* welfare theory, which is largely concerned with demonstrating the optimal properties of free competition and the unfettered price system, is undoubtedly due to its elegance and simplicity. Admit the existence of external effects, and both disappear. Even under ideal circumstances, price no longer measures the marginal contribution a good makes to social welfare—it measures the contribution it makes to private welfare, which may be something quite different. We have to retreat to banal statements about social rates of indifference, and can say virtually nothing that could ever have any practical bearing on problems of the day.

Must we then conclude that Pigou was wrong when he claimed that 'The complicated analyses which economists endeavour to carry through are not mere gymnastic. They are instruments for the bettering of human life'? † I do not think that we must. But I do feel very strongly that the greatest contribution economics is likely to make to human welfare, broadly conceived, is through *positive* studies—through contributing to our understanding of how the economic system actually works in practice—rather than through normative welfare theory itself.

If positive economics can provide people with an understanding of the various far-reaching indirect effects of particular policies, it will probably also provide them with a basis for drawing welfare conclusions, for themselves and according to their own lights. In my view the job of the economist is not to try to reach welfare conclusions for others, but rather to make available the positive knowledge—the information and the understanding—on the basis of which laymen (and economists themselves, out of office hours) can pass judgement.

It is for this reason that I choose to regard aggregate index numbers of output or consumption as mere providers of information which may or may not be useful in themselves, but which are

† A. C. Pigou, *The Economics of Welfare* (3rd ed., London, 1928), preface.

certainly devoid of normative significance. One of the tasks of theoretical economics is then simply to *predict* what particular index numbers will be in the future (or explain why they were what they were in the past), and not to say what they ought to be if welfare is to be maximized.

Similarly, the economist cannot say at what level the National Coal Board should set the price of coal. He can merely make clear (or attempt to make clear) the probable consequences of setting it at various different levels. If he succeeds in this task it will almost certainly become more widely appreciated that tinkering with the price mechanism is one of the more feasible and generally satisfactory ways of securing whatever distribution of wealth is desired.

No doubt many professional economists are reluctant to abdicate what they may like to regard as their traditional prescriptive role, and are uneasy at the prospect of becoming mere purveyors of information. If they are, it is up to them to show how welfare economics can be set upon a basis which is even reasonably satisfactory—or can be made to yield conclusions with which a significant number of men are likely to concur.

INDEX OF AUTHORS

INDEX OF SUBJECTS